REALITY TV

Reality TV is popular entertainment. And yet a common way to start a conversation about it is 'I wouldn't want anyone to know this but ... '. Why do people love, and love to hate, reality TV?

This book explores reality TV in all its forms – from competitive talent shows to reality soaps – examining a range of programmes from the mundane to those that revel in the spectacle of excess. Annette Hill's research draws on interviews with television producers on the market of reality TV and audience research involving over 15,000 participants during a 15-year period.

Key themes in the book include: the phenomenon of reality TV as a new kind of inter-generic space; the rise of reality entertainment formats and producer intervention; audiences, fans and anti-fans; the spectacle of reality and sports entertainment; and the ways real people and celebrities perform themselves in cross-media content.

Reality TV explores how this form of popular entertainment invites audiences to riff on reality, to debate and reject reality claims, making it ideal for students of media and cultural studies seeking a broader understanding of how media connects with trends in society and culture.

Annette Hill is a Professor of Media at Lund University, Sweden. Her research focuses on audiences, with interests in media experiences, everyday life, genres and cultures of viewing. Her most recent book is *Paranormal Media* (2011). Her next book is *Media Experiences* (2016).

KEY IDEAS IN MEDIA AND CULTURAL STUDIES

The *Key Ideas in Media and Cultural Studies* series covers the main concepts, issues, debates and controversies in contemporary media and cultural studies. Titles in the series constitute authoritative, original essays rather than literary surveys, but are also written explicitly to support undergraduate teaching. The series provides students and teachers with lively and original treatments of key topics in the field.

Cultural Policy by David Bell and Kate Oakley

Reality TV by Annette Hill

Forthcoming:

Culture by Ben Highmore

Celebrity by Sean Redmond

Representation by Jenny Kidd

Mediatization by Andreas Hepp

REALITY TV

Annette Hill

Routledge
Taylor & Francis Group

LONDON AND NEW YORK

First published 2015
by Routledge
2 Park Square, Milton Park, Abingdon, Oxon, OX14 4RN

and by Routledge
711 Third Avenue, New York, NY 10017

Routledge is an imprint of the Taylor & Francis Group, an informa business

British Library Cataloguing in Publication Data
A catalogue record for this book is available from the British Library

Library of Congress Cataloging-in-Publication Data
Hill, Annette.
Reality TV / Annette Hill.
pages cm. – (Key ideas in media and cultural studies)
Includes bibliographical references and index.
1. Reality television programs–History and criticism. I. Title.
PN1992.8.R43H55 2014
791.45'6–dc23
2014023004

ISBN: 978-0-415-69175-8 (hbk)
ISBN: 978-0-415-69176-5 (pbk)
ISBN: 978-0-203-08219-5 (ebk)

Typeset in Garamond
by Taylor & Francis Books

MIX
Paper from
responsible sources
FSC
www.fsc.org   FSC® C013056

Printed and bound in Great Britain by
TJ International Ltd, Padstow, Cornwall

To Peter, who has a big heart, and to my family and friends for their warm embrace.

Contents

List of figures viii
Acknowledgements ix

1 **Introduction: Reality TV** 1

2 **Big Brother moment** 24

3 **Performance of the self** 52

4 **Reality TV experiences** 80

5 **Reality and sports entertainment** 104

6 **Conclusion: Reality bites** 137

Appendix 166
References 168
Index 179

FIGURES

1.1 Reality TV embedded in everyday life.   2
1.2 *Idol* game in second-hand shop.   18
5.1 Wrestling as spectacle of excess.   105
5.2 Hushing mime (Dan Ahtola).   108
6.1 Mime and clown (Dan Ahtola and Eddie Vega).   151

Acknowledgements

This book is based on over 15 years of research on reality television. Some ideas for the book first appeared in *Reality TV* (2004) and *Restyling Factual TV* (2007) and I thank Routledge, and Natalie Foster, for encouraging me to write this book for the Key Ideas series. An early version of ideas presented in Chapter 4 on reality TV experiences was first published in Ouellette, Laurie, ed. (2014) *A Companion to Reality Television*, Malden, MA and Oxford, UK: Wiley Blackwell. Thank you for permission to use parts of my chapter from that edited collection.

For details of the projects and funding bodies that are referred to in the book see the Appendix. In particular, I would like to thank the former Broadcasting Standards Commission and Independent Television Commission, the Office of Communications, the Economic and Social Research Council, the University of Westminster, Lund University, and the Marianne and Marcus Wallenbergs Foundation for research support and funding. For research on professional wrestling, I would like to thank Michael Rübsamen for introducing me to the whole thing, and Dan Ahtola for his generosity in participating in the research. I would also like to thank Michael Rübsamen and Fredrik Schoug for permission to reproduce their photographs of wrestling. A special thank you to my colleagues in Media and Communication at Lund University, and two heads of department Patrik Lundell and Tobias Olsson for their research support. In particular, a special thank you to Ian Calcutt, Peter Dahlgren, Tina Askanius and Joanna Doona for their ongoing encouragement.

Several people agreed to be interviewed for the book, so thank you to Dan Ahtola, Gary Carter, John Corner, Julie Donovan, Pål Hollender, Jane Roscoe and Douglas Wood for their generosity and perceptive comments. I would also like to thank the anonymous readers who commented on the book proposal, and John Corner, Jane Roscoe and Gary Carter for their detailed suggestions and advice for the final manuscript. Finally, a big thank you goes out to all the people who participated in various projects from the 1990s until now. These participants are the real stars of the book.

1

INTRODUCTION
REALITY TV

You take it with a pinch of salt.

(19-year-old female student)

'It's a phenomenon' (BBC 2011). When people say reality TV is a phenomenon they are referring to the sheer scale and sweep of shows and formats that are a big part of everyday life. Reality TV is often more talked about than watched. A global format like *Got Talent* (Syco and FremantleMedia) attracts millions of viewers to live shows in countries around the world, many more millions download and share YouTube clips, and even more people chat about the show. A small-scale reality soap like *The Only Way is Essex* (ITV2, UK) can attract more Twitter followers than viewers. A studio-based show like *Dancing on Ice* with an average audience of eight million (ITV1, UK) is considered a failure if it doesn't make tabloid headlines. Reality TV is caught up in what is happening now. Individual shows, news headlines, social media trends and even big events date very quickly. Try watching last season's finale of *American Idol* (Fox, USA); it just lacks presence. But as live phenomena, reality TV makes a mark.

Figure 1.1 Reality TV embedded in everyday life. Photograph: Annette Hill.

It is no mean feat to make a mark in today's media landscape. The world is littered with failed films, television shows, music, magazines, mobile apps and websites. And reality TV is no exception. For every successful format like *Strictly Come Dancing* (BBC Worldwide) there are many failures. Producers say content is king. But with reality TV, this is not always the case. As this viewer said '*The X-Factor*, *I'm a Celebrity* … just rubbish really, but I think I've watched all of them' (23-year-old female shop assistant).

For example, *Splash!* (Eyeworks) is a reality show about diving. *Time*'s TV critic named it one of the top ten worst TV shows of 2013: 'some reality shows achieve brilliance by embracing ridiculousness. This awkward, unpleasant diving competition just bellyflopped straight into it' (Poniewozik 2013). Despite dire reviews, *Splash!* still had 4.4 million American viewers on ABC for its finale, four million more than expected for a show about celebrities jumping into water (Hibberd 2013a). In the UK, the first episode attracted five million viewers on ITV1. This TV critic wrote: 'It's almost certainly going to be awful, and you almost certainly won't be able to stop watching it' (Heritage 2013c). It became a source of gossip for people, tabloid headlines, celebrity magazines and social media – '*Splash!* becomes our TV guilty pleasure' (*Daily Mail* 2013).

Reality TV is often shorthand for what people think is wrong with modern culture – time wasting, low grade, rubbish. Writer Seth Kaufman (2013) explains: '[R]eality TV is the most commercially successful format in the most dominant marketing medium in history ... this mutating, low-cost, high-ratings, often low brow, train wreck of a genre is everywhere.' Everyone has something to say about it. Take this comment: '[T]o each one's own, but take reality TV as far away from me as possible. I have much more enlightening ways of wasting my time' (Brache 2013). Or this viewer: reality TV 'is like putting two insects together in a jar and seeing what happens ... You know it is very primitive' (56-year-old male freelance researcher).

Not all reality TV is seen as bad. There are shows that garner critical acclaim. Choir master Gareth Malone is 'Michael Palin's only serous rival for the title of the nicest man on TV' (Lawson 2012). In *Military Wives* (BBC2 2011), Malone coached untrained singers into the first military wives' choir in Britain; the choir's first song became the UK's Christmas number one (2011). *MasterChef* (Shine Group) is an international format with a winning combination of critically acclaimed chefs as judges and passionate cooks as competitors. One viewer said of *MasterChef*, the amateur version: '[I]t's a chance to see real people shine on TV' (60-year-old female teacher). But most of the time reality television has come to mean popular entertainment. When a character in the novel *Moonlight Mile* (Lehane 2010: 7) comments on 'some soul-crushing reality show about stupid people' we know what they mean.

Some people love reality shows. Other people love to hate reality TV. In a poll for *The Hollywood Reporter* (2012) *American Idol's* Ryan Seacrest was voted 'both the most beloved, and loathed, reality TV host'. Gary Carter (2014), Chairman of Northern Europe, Chairman of 360° Shine Group, comments:

> [T]his ambiguity is reflected in the industry too. The relatively low/ambiguous status of the reality series is evidenced by the fact that there is only one Primetime Emmy given to reality as a genre, in a prize run-down dominated by drama.

When reality events like *I'm a Celebrity* ... (ITV1, UK) are running every night during an intense few weeks you can eavesdrop on conversations everywhere, from gossip at the shops, to radio and second screen chatter. Even reality refuseniks have plenty to say on the subject. For example this viewer noted 'thousands of so-called reality programmes. These are devastating television programmes to the detriment of viewing. It is a descent into the pit' (65-year-old retired male). You don't have to watch reality TV to have an opinion about it.

If we visualize the value of reality TV as a cultural phenomenon we would see shows overshadowed by talk about them. In a representative sample of 4,516 people (aged 16–65+) in Britain in 2003 only 15 per cent thought it important reality programmes were shown on TV (Hill 2007). Still, nearly 60 per cent admitted to watching the genre. As this person explained: there is 'crap I would never watch, crap I might watch, and then crap I would definitely watch' (33-year-old male student). Clearly, reality TV has entertainment value for audiences otherwise it wouldn't dominate the primetime schedules in the way it does. But people don't watch or talk about shows in the same way as drama, for example. Favourite drama series inspire devotion from dedicated fans. When a reality soap beat dramas such as *Downton Abbey* (ITV1, UK) and *Sherlock* (BBC1, UK) to a BAFTA YouTube Audience Award (2011) critics worried about the future of entertainment television. The look of shock on actor Martin Freeman's face (*Sherlock*) as the award was announced became a YouTube hit in itself, with many people watching that moment rather than the award ceremony or the reality soap. One person commented after the announcement of the award: 'I'm not going to say the people on *The Only Way is Essex* are representative of everything that's wrong with modern culture, but I'm sure going to think it loudly' (*Guardian* 2011). A similar turning point occurred in America with *Duck Dynasty* (A&E 2014, USA), when it beat *American Idol* and *Survivor* in the ratings for the key demographic of 18–59 year olds (O'Connell 2014).

Göran Bolin notes the value of media can be found not so much in content but in how value is produced from that content (2011). The value of reality television often lies beyond the content on offer. For example, the value of mega format *Idols* is about its economic value as an international entertainment format, its aesthetic value as live entertainment for cross-media content, and its cultural, or social, value. The connections across these different types of value are constantly shifting positions. When Simon Fuller had the idea for *Pop Idol* in the early 2000s, his idea became a format that was rolled out globally as a reality talent show. According to the official FremantleMedia (2014) website, *Idols* has been 'watched by over 460 million viewers worldwide since it first launched in 2001' and 'the *Idols* format has aired 207 series across 47 territories to date'. According to the *New York Times* (Stelter 2012), the 2012 season of *American Idol* saw the format 'grappling with its own competition'. This season had an average of 19.2 million viewers, with 7.9 million viewers aged 18–49; the ratings were down on previous years with an average of over 20 million viewers, and 10 million in the coveted 18–49 age group. Rival talent shows challenged the juggernaut, although *American Idol* still remained number one after eleven seasons on Fox. TV critics and social media chatter suggested the series had lost its cultural value, suffering from format fatigue. A commentator for the (now defunct) website Television Without Pity noted how contestants 'probably can't remember a world without *American Idol*', training for the competition from a young age – 'it's like watching somebody who was grown in a vat for this purpose' (Stelter 2012). For 2013, the season dropped its pole position by 40 per cent compared to 2012, with 14.3 million viewers, in particular losing younger viewers. The average audience age is around 50: 'it's become your grandparents' *American Idol*' (Halperin 2013). For 2014, the ratings dropped further, with 8.4 million for a mid-March show. The ratings decline marks 'the fall of the house of "Idol"' (Carter 2014).

What makes people say reality TV is a phenomenon is something hard to qualify. It is 'the moment' that everyone talks about. This moment is priceless. It is what makes viewers tune in, vote, share, gossip, buy and return to a show. Some commentators call this moment a cultural zeitgeist. Reality TV had this moment around the turn of the millennium with the start of *Big*

Brother (Endemol) and the rise of competitive reality. Lawson (2014) argues:

> Series such as *The X Factor*, *Big Brother* and (in America) *Survivor* have exposed a brutality and cruelty that was not previously part of television and was not as explicitly present in human nature. So the rise of these violently divisive entertainments is a genuine cultural phenomenon.

For example Chuck Palahniuk's *Haunted* (2005) is a satire of reality television about writers in residence who lock themselves in an abandoned theatre for three months, turning their lives into a 'true life horror story with a happy ending'. He writes: 'The difference between how you look and how you see yourself is enough to kill most people' (Palahniuk 2005: 144).

According to Jane Roscoe, Head of SBS international sales:

> Reality TV has led the way, but dramas are the formats of the now. Reality TV has done so much to change how the industry works, and that is always fascinating. But, where are the shows that still make us say 'oh that is great'?

A show that makes us say 'great!' is drama series *The Walking Dead* (AMC 2010–), based on graphic novels. The series averaged 19.9 million viewers per episode in 2013, with many in the 18–49 age range, beating most other series and sports events on American television. According to *Entertainment Weekly*: 'The *Walking Dead*'s ratings are big. Like really, really big' (Hibberd 2013b). The *New York Times* noted: 'The Walking Dead is officially devouring the rest of television ... before Sunday night, every top-rated show this season had been an N.F.L. game. Now zombies are apparently more appealing than quarterbacks' (Carter 2013). Perhaps, the cultural zeitgeist of the moment is being 'post alive'. As Chuck Palahniuk notes in his latest novel: 'when you die, trust me, the most difficult person to leave behind is yourself' (Palahniuk 2013: 33).

In short, we can say reality TV is a phenomenon in the sense that it is part of a social and media matrix. 'It is not possible to understand reality TV unless it can be connected to something else' (Bignell 2005: 177). We can understand reality television as a broad generic phenomenon that makes a mark as popular entertainment. And we can understand it as individual series that have phenomenal moments that grab audience/user attention. At this moment in time reality television is also a fading phenomenon. The elements that have made it part of a cultural zeitgeist are now a little tired and repetitive. It is a challenge for reality television to refresh itself with new formats and series that make people say 'that is great!'

What this means for a book about reality TV is a focus on its role in broader debates within popular culture, in social, political and cultural contexts. Specifically this book explores how reality television is a situated phenomenon. A central argument is that it is not possible to understand reality TV unless it is connected to audiences. People are crucial actors in the multistage drama of a cultural phenomenon. This is not to deny the power of producers, participants, celebrities, advertisers and distributors, just some of the professionals behind the making of reality TV (see Ouellette 2014), or to ignore the significance of aesthetics, narrative, characterization, sound and editing, to list some of the ways reality is represented (see Lury 2005). Nor can we disregard wider themes of consumerism or class, the politics of surveillance and the state, or the morals and ethics of fairness and respect, to mention a few of the salient political and social issues running through reality television shows (see Kraidy and Sender 2011). What can be said is that the production, aesthetics and politics of reality TV are connected to audiences and publics, consumers and producers, participants and users, fans and anti-fans, readers, listeners, viewers – all these people and their practices.

This book argues that reality TV producers, participants and audiences co-create cultural experiences, events and trends. For Gary Carter (2014) 'reality television is a genre of non-scripted entertainment: genres are also co-created'. The idea of a co-creation of producer, participant and audience practices is a term that is situated within political economics and production studies, where structural factors are a basis for producer–market–consumer relations. And it is a term that is situated within audience studies, where media content can be used as cultural resources for understanding agency, identity and power. We should be wary of using a term like co-creation without qualifying both the structural factors that can lead to political interpretations of the media production–consumer relations, and the resource factors that can lead to cultural interpretations of production–audience relations. Rather than see co-creation as a cooperative endeavour, it is often a tense relationship between different groups of people who are engaged in multiple practices. To that end, the term 'reality' relations is used to signal the connections between producer, participant and audience practices.

Viviana Zelizer in her book *The Purchase of Intimacy* (2005) calls the mingling of economic activity and social relations 'connected lives'. 'People are continually involved in maintaining, reinforcing, testing, and sometimes challenging their relations to each other' (2005: 306). For Zelizer: 'there is not one strategic actor moving against another. Instead, we find people locating themselves within webs of social relations' (ibid.). This idea of connected lives is suggestive of the ways producer–audience practices can be located within economic and social or cultural contexts. This is not one power player moving against another, but people maintaining, reinforcing, testing and challenging the 'reality' relations between each other in a push–pull dynamic.

The 'reality' relations between producers and audiences are complex practices. For every successful format that becomes a talking point there are many failures. For all the preparation by producers in the staging of a reality event there are still a dozen ways audiences can react in unforeseen circumstances. According to one viewer: 'these programmes are created by us. We create demand for them, we create the justification for them, we create their success and we create therefore their continuity. So, we can't blame them for what we want them to do' (34-year-old male mobile phone seller). The success and continuity of reality television as a phenomenon is situated in these 'reality' relations between producers, participants and audiences.

DEFINITIONS

The act of defining reality TV is not easy. It is a moving target and there are different definitions of it as fact and entertainment by the industry and critics, scholars and audiences. 'Reality TV is a nodal point at which different discourses within and outside television culture have temporarily come together in an unstable conjunction' (Bignell 2005: 171). Unstable conjunctions, different discourses, all signal something tricky about reality TV. It resists a single identity, occupying multiple positions for different groups of people, in various regions and cultures.

Reality television is a container for a range of diverse programmes, series, formats and events in which elements of documentary, talent shows, gameshows, talkshows, soap operas, melodramas and sports mix together to produce sub-genres. According to John Corner (2014), 'reality television is a new kind of inter-generic space rather than a genre'. We can broadly define reality television into two distinct spaces that draw on various sub-variants of other genres across fact, drama and entertainment. There is the 'world' space of television programmes set in hospitals, airports or hotels. Many examples of the 'world' space of reality television can be found in early forms of factual entertainment in the 1990s, such as docusoaps, or crime and emergency programming. Today, series such as *A Very British Airline* (BBC 2014) or *Duck Dynasty* tend to be set in real-world spaces, and are often described as 'fly on the wall', 'docusoap' or 'reality soap' to signal the mix of observational-style documentary and soap opera elements within this style of reality television. The inter-generic space of these series and formats set in real-world locations usually contain participants who are performing as themselves in recognizable social roles, such as parent or airline worker. Sometimes these series are based around a celebrity, like that of the series built around the actress Lindsay Lohan. This kind of reality television is often deeply banal, although that does not mean to say it is any less engaging to viewers. Reality television as 'world' space was dominant in the 1990s, and in the last few years has seen a resurgence as a primetime ratings hit with younger audiences.

The other kind of reality content includes the 'television' space of programmes set in specially designed studios, houses or locations. Many examples of the 'television' space of reality television can be found in competitive reality such as *Big Brother* and *Survivor*, talent shows such as *Pop Idol* or *Strictly Come Dancing*, and cookery shows like *MasterChef*. These programmes are all formats, and have proved to be very successful business models in the development of reality television for cross-media content. This type of reality television is usually described as 'shiny floor shows', 'talent contests', 'lifestyle' and 'factual entertainment' to signal the mix of entertainment, talkshows or sports competition within these formats. The inter-generic space of these series and formats set in created for television locations usually contain participants as contestants who are both performing as themselves and competing in a reality contest. Often these formats contain celebrities and professional dancers, singers or music producers, or there are celebrity versions of the formats that work alongside amateur versions. This kind of reality television is often a spectacle of excess, although this does not mean to say it is never banal. These kinds of reality entertainment formats have dominated global television for the past 15 years, and it is only in the last few years that the series are suffering from format fatigue. For this reason, the book focuses on this kind of reality television as popular and often spectacular entertainment in order to understand the development of reality TV as an inter-generic space. The concluding chapter offers suggestions for the next phase of its generic development.

If we look back in time, early studies struggled to come up with an agreed definition, some scholars settling for popular factual entertainment, others infotainment. Industry professionals sometimes used factual entertainment to describe a popularizing trend in fact-based programming. The term was not value free. A documentary commissioning department wouldn't want to draw attention to its factual entertainment hits, for example. But still, the slim separation of the terms factual and entertainment lent an air of respectability to this kind of media content. There were some facts, some foundation in actuality even if *Rescue 911* (CBS 1989–96, USA) or its UK equivalent *999* (BBC 1992–2003) did rely on an 'aesthetics of attraction' (Corner 1996). BBC producers argued that 999 was not entirely entertainment based, attempting to teach the public first aid tips (Hill 2000a). *Big Brother* was originally promoted as a social experiment, although contestants chanted 'it's only a gameshow' (Mathijs 2002). Factual entertainment is still a useful definition today, covering a broad range of cross-media content within a variety of genres, like documentary, lifestyle and light entertainment. The title of the book *Consuming Reality: the Commercialisation of Factual Entertainment* (Deery 2012) tells the reader marketing and consumer trends, like advertising and branding, run across a range of factual and entertainment content.

Academics sometimes used infotainment as a definition, merging two established areas of investigation – in media as information and media as entertainment – into one focus of study on the downward spiral of news as spectacle. Articles like 'Who's Afraid of Infotainment?' (Brants 1998), or books such as *Tabloid Culture* (Glynn 2000) addressed concerns regarding the commercial imperatives of news, sidelining accurate information about current events or world politics in favour of sensational stories and celebrity gossip. Although the history of news is replete with examples of an 'aesthetics of attraction' to sell newspapers to the general public, studies on infotainment represented a growing area of scholarship that recognized tabloid tendencies such as character-driven news, or emotional journalism, running rife not only in newspapers, but also in primetime television. The term was laden with negative value judgements. Infotainment was a definition for 'lowest common denominator' news or television, and as such something to resist and critique.

Audiences referred to infotainment, or factual entertainment on occasion, preferring to use whatever description came to hand at the moment of conversation, such as 'people programmes', 'normal life stuff', 'fly on the wall stuff' (Hill 2005). 'Stuff' summed up the difficulty people had in describing a diverse number of programmes that mixed fact with fiction – 'what happens and stuff' (16-year-old female student). Throughout the 1990s different kinds of programmes peaked viewers' attention, from high-speed car chases and acute medical conditions, to the slower pace of work on a cruise ship and learning to drive a car. There were emergency services programmes where cameras followed crime and health professionals on the job (see Hill 2000a, 2000b). There were docusoaps where cameras followed ordinary people on the job at airports or hotels (see Dovey 2000). Both of these types of reality television popularized news (on the scene as it happens) and documentary (fly on the wall) though mixing factual genres with other more dramatic or entertaining ones like soap opera or lifestyle (see Kilborn 2003). These shows were very popular, attracting at their peak up to half of the audience share at the time of transmission. Audiences sometimes used value-laden terms like 'car crash TV' or 'tabloid TV' to signal their critical take on this kind of television. But more often than not people talked about the titles of programmes and the times they were scheduled on TV. Throughout the 1990s there was no clear-cut definition of all these shows about 'what happens and stuff'.

The term reality TV was around in the late 1980s and 1990s in reference to police and emergency services series or MTV's *The Real World* (1992–) but it wasn't by any means the dominant definition in everyday talk about these kinds of programmes. Unlike talkshows that were fully established by the 1990s, reality TV had yet to settle into popular consciousness as a recognizable term. Critics wrote about 'reality-based programming', invariably with a scathing attack on the channels that hawked such poor quality stuff, or the news presenters who fronted sensationalist shows about speeding cars, bloody accidents and noisy neighbours. One academic study on actuality in popular documentary called it 'reality' television, the quote marks signaling an uncertainty in the use of the word real (Kilborn 1994); another on the political economic background to series like *Cops* on Fox (1998–2013, USA) called this new form 'reali-TV', showing an even greater hesitation in coupling reality with this kind of programming (Raphael 1997). Similarly, audiences would add caveats like 'sort of almost reality' to show their awareness of the slipperiness of the term. Jeffrey Sconce called reality TV 'our new genre of hesitation, thrilling us with its confusion of once distinct realms' (2004: 264). Such hesitation could be heard in the very term reality TV.

The hesitancy surrounding what to call this new cultural for-mation in the 1990s changed after the global success of reality entertainment formats such as *Big Brother* (Endemol) and *Survivor* (Planet 24, Castaway). Along came a new hybrid format that did not follow people around but instead created a scenario for the cameras. Reality gameshows mixed news, documentary, soap opera, gameshows and sports to create a successful format that could be sold around the world. This period was also the time when reality TV crossed the borders between television, radio, newspapers, magazines, mobiles and the internet, with content on all platforms (see Holmes and Jermyn 2004, Murray and Ouell-ette 2004). It was truly a new phenomenon in the business of making media (Bazalgette 2005).

Simply put, a format is a way of taking a creative idea, like the reality gameshow *Big Brother* and formatting that idea as a series made in different countries and regions. In an article on reality entertainment formats, the fashion term 'made to measure' was used to convey the way formats have a certain pattern that can be adjusted for different regions (Hill and Steemers 2011). The rea-lity formats of the 2000s are household names worldwide (see Kraidy and Sender 2011). There are live formats that recruit public votes for each media event (*The X Factor*), and pre-recorded formats that mobilize audience attention and public debate through the scheduling of the series (*MasterChef*). Reality formats utilize all kinds of cross-media content. The formats rely on the mothership of the television programme, linked to votes via tele-phones, mobiles and second screens, audience interaction via live events and social media, and public debate on radio, and in newspapers and magazines (see Oren and Shahaf 2012). The big-gest formats have spin-off events, like a sister programme that focuses on gossip and interviews with contestants and judges, a national tour or a reunion show, and extra products, like mobile applications, games and songs. These global formats span a variety of themes including survival competitions like *I'm a Celebrity ...* , talent competitions like *The X Factor*, cooking competitions like *Hell's Kitchen* (ITV Studios) and business competitions like *The Apprentice* (Mark Burnett Productions). The roll-out of a format like *Idols* across the media landscape, in each country or region, is a professionally managed juggernaut. This is reality TV as an entertainment genre.

Reality TV has become the default definition for a media mix of factual entertainment. Within the industry, the term signals both the market for international entertainment formats and for smaller-scale productions aimed at local audiences. Big reality formats grab ratings and appeal to a wide range of audiences. Smaller reality soaps, or more localized formats, can bolster a minority channel, and have modest success. For example Boyle and Kelly show how business reality TV has a 'double demographic'. In an interview entrepreneur Doug Richard describes the show *Dragons' Den* on BBC2 as appealing to the traditional, older, more upmarket audience for the channel and also to younger viewers with an interest in how to get on in the world of business (2012: 45). Boyle and Kelly write that reality TV 'offers an insight into wider television industry shifts as producers (both independent and in-house) have moved from addressing a fairly captive analogue audience towards engaging with a more restless viewership in the digital age' (2012: 46). By drawing on fact and fiction, industry professionals can use the mix to attract a double demographic, indeed often multiplying their success across a diversity of viewers in different countries. *The Great British Bake Off* (BBC) is a perfect example of a factual entertainment mix, blending a cookery competition with a strong set of characters and storylines, appealing to a double demographic, and appearing in other countries as a format – *Hela Sverige Bakar* (Shine, Nordic, TV4, Sweden).

Many scholars use the term reality TV to stand in for a wider set of enquiries about a cultural formation constantly on the move. For example Van Bauwel and Carpentier consider reality TV as a meta genre that 'raises questions about the status of representation and reality in contemporary societies' (2010: 6). The very blurring of the boundaries between fact and fiction makes the genre 'trans-reality', a term they describe as stretching the notion of reality to something constructed within media and society. Other research has examined a migrating genre where there is a 'complex interplay among the meanings of nation, gender, class, celebrity, politics and globalism on the terrain marked out by reality television' (Sender 2011: 3). Here, reality TV is a carrier for theories, ideas and values that shift across a global mediascape. There is also research that uses reality television as a marker point for major change. For example Boyle and Kelly analyse business reality TV like *The Apprentice* as part of wider structural changes in the media industry and political economic changes in society as a whole. The notion of the celebrity entrepreneur is situated in a 'wider matrix of media discourses through which people acquire ideas and knowledge about society more generally' (2012: 2).

Perhaps the people most in tune with reality TV today are audiences. After all, audiences are the experts, in the sense that they watch, consume and gossip about reality television more than anyone else. For audiences the genre is a mix of entertainment and information, in that order. In a survey of British audiences in 2003, more than half of respondents in a representative survey of 4,516 (aged 16–65+) claimed reality TV was entertaining rather than informative (61 per cent for formats like *Big Brother*, 53 per cent for formats like *Faking It*) (see Hill 2007). Such a view of reality TV as entertainment with some facts in the mix is only going to be more prevalent today, as the juggernaut of talent formats like *Strictly Come Dancing* (BBC Worldwide) continue to dominate primetime. Structured reality shows, or reality soaps, place the dramatic element very much to the foreground in this kind of television. Participants in *Mob Wives* (VH1 2011–, USA) talk openly in interviews of having characters and storylines. The sense that 'reality TV has come to mean anything with somebody who isn't a trained actor in it' (26-year-old male office worker) has shifted to include both celebrities and also professional reality TV contestants. When Rob Kardashian from *Keeping up with the Kardashians* (E!, 2007–, USA) appeared in *Dancing with the Stars* (ABC 2011) he was introduced as a reality TV star. The attitude of audiences to reality TV today is best summed up by this quote from a viewer: 'You take it with a pinch of salt' (19-year-old female student).

If we take a moment to look beyond reality television there are examples of the category as factual entertainment used in the promotion of, and inspiration for, literature, theatre and tourism.

The King of Pain by Seth Kaufman (2012) is a satire about a pro-ducer of a torture-themed reality show, based in part on what the author calls 'enter-pain-ments' like *Survivor* and *Jersey* ('Hell is other people') *Shore* and 'the dismal, non critical, exploitative, voyeur-vision, Honey Boo Boo state of reality television' (Kaufman 2013). Sebastian Faulks in the novel *A Week in December* (2009) satirizes reality formats in the modern comedy show *It's Madness,* where patients with bipolar disorder, for example, are chosen by a panel of celebrity judges to spend a weekend under the scrutiny of hidden cameras in Barking Bungalow. 'Television is a con – everyone knew that – but *It's Madness* worked because, in the words of the programme makers, it was "there to make people think differently, to challenge their preconceptions"' (2009: 42). Faulks critiques reality TV and its audience through the character of Finn, an adolescent boy who likes to watch *It's Madness* whilst having a 'massive high'. Finn suffers a psychotic attack and, like the patients in the show, tries 'with all his childish might to keep a grip on a reality he could no longer properly inhabit' (2009: 98).

I Dreamed a Dream is a theatre musical based on the rise to fame of Susan Boyle, a contestant on *Britain's Got Talent* in 2009 who sang this song in her audition and became a worldwide hit on YouTube. In 2010 her debut album *I Dreamed a Dream* made it into the Guinness World Records for the fastest-selling album by a UK female. *Viva Forever!* is a musical that satirizes *The X Factor*, using songs from the Spice Girls back catalogue. It was conceived by Judy Craymer, originator of global hit *Mamma Mia!*, and written by comedian Jennifer Saunders. Craymer said:

> We set out to create a contemporary story that truly reflects our time; to take a satirical look at the underbelly of a TV talent show and the chaos that ensues for a mother, her daughter and their friends; a theatrical event to embrace all generations both on and off the stage.
> (Sherwin 2013)

The show lasted six months in London's West End before having to close in 2013 with losses of millions. Another reality satire musical, *I Can't Sing! The X Factor Musical*, only lasted two months before closing its doors.

According to Fox News (Piazza 2011) 'Towns and Tourist Sites Get a Bump on Success of TV Shows'. The hamlet of Seaside in New Jersey saw a rise in visitors after *Jersey Shore* (MTV 2009–12) with the series receiving tax credits from the state for its contribution to the local economy. When *The Bachelorette* filmed in Fiji (ABC 2011), travel operator Down Under Answers claimed, 'The public truly became engaged with Fiji during and after the airing of *The Bachelorette*, and we've seen a tremendous growth in our Fiji business'. Former star of *The Bachelor* Jason Mesnick and his wife Molly capitalized on this tourism destination by appearing as part of a cruise: 'for *Bachelor* fans it was a fun chance for people to hang out with us and they get to say, "hey, I saw this place on TV and it looks pretty great"' (quoted in Piazza 2011). In an article titled 'How Reality Television Shapes Travel' the Hilton's Bora Bora Nui Resort and Spa told how it increased its occupancy by 55 per cent after hosting the format in 2010: '*The Bachelorette* is practically a travelogue.' The hotel also hosts other reality TV performers: 'If you host the Kardashians at your hotel, you know it's going to be in *US Weekly* and *People* every week' (Norris 2012). These examples highlight the branding of places and personalities within reality TV shows and related tourism experiences, what June Deery describes as 'the embedding of commercial agenda into experience' (2012: 2).

In point of fact, you come across reality TV embedded in the most everyday environments. There is a board game for *Pop Idol*, with six playing pieces, a *Pop Idol* star, dice and instructions for players to provide their favourite CD. At time of writing you can buy from Amazon a new *Pop Idol* boardgame for GBP 39.99 (only one left in stock), or a second-hand one for GPB 14.99. There's a *Pop Idol* boardgame in a charity shop for less than a pound. When auditions for *Sverige Idol* (TV4 2011) took place in Lund, Sweden queues began the day before, people camping out to be first in line. As they queued, friends and family jollied everyone along with picnics, bottles of beer and wine, and impromptu singalongs. Only a few were serious about their audition, most were doing it to say they had been there. Many recorded themselves on mobile phones, sharing their experience of being in the *Idol* queue. As the day came to a close, crows picked at the debris left

Figure 1.2 Idol game in a second-hand shop. Photograph: Annette Hill.

behind by the people from the *Idol* auditions. This is the thing – reality TV starts out as a phenomenon and quickly becomes yesterday's news.

AUDIENCE RESEARCH

On a personal note, I have been studying reality TV audiences since the 1990s to the present day. I draw on this data for different projects, at different times, to tell the evolving story of reality television and audiences. This book argues for understanding reality TV in relation to audiences. This argument is fuelled by the knowledge that audiences are usually absent from debates about reality TV, whether in the press, in academic studies or in the industry. In the 1990s, when reality TV took off as a genre in America, Australia and Europe, audiences were usually caricatured as dumb, or as voyeurs. There was industry data on audiences and consumers, from ratings statistics to in-house studies of target groups. But, if you followed the press reports, or looked at early academic studies, there were plenty of assertions but very few studies that involved people who actually watched reality TV. Perhaps reality TV was thought to be too popular to warrant the time and energy it takes to study audiences.

By the 2000s, there was an explosion in reality TV formats and academic studies began to take into account discourses of audiences, voting revenues, ratings data and representations of people within the media. Now you can find studies of reality TV and global formats offering a wide range of interpretations, from the globalization of reality TV to political issues embedded in reality TV events or scandals, from gender, class and nation to the mediation of reality more generally across television, news and social media. Given the wealth of studies on reality TV today, and the richness of interpretations on offer, it is surprising that audiences are still largely absent from this story. Still, there are assertions about audiences, or caricatures of audiences, as dupes, zombies or celebrity wannabes. Claims about reality TV need to be investigated by also talking to audiences, consumers and users, participants and performers, listening and observing people to understand their perspectives.

Joke Hermes notes 'the aim of audience studies is to give voice to groups of audience members' (2012: 198). Her comment can be understood both in relation to a democratization, or knowledge, project and also an entertainment project. In terms of democratization, voice can mean a plurality of public voices within a model of deliberative democracy (Couldry 2010). Here, the media is a resource for a democratization project, whereby newspapers, or television, provides knowledge to citizens so they can participate in civil society. Stephen Coleman and Karen Ross point out the role of the media in representing publics, so that citizens can see and hear themselves within public spheres, a collective made up of diverse individuals and groups (2010). In terms of entertainment, voice can mean multiple identities of individuals and groups within the shared space of popular culture. Here, the media is a resource for an entertainment project, whereby television drama, or the internet, provides experiences for audiences and consumers to understand their identities, or interpret media content in relation to their own personal lives. It is this meaning of voice that is more relevant to this book and its analysis of reality television as popular entertainment. For a more political analysis of reality television see Kraidy and Sender (2011), amongst others.

How audience researchers give voice to subjects is not without difficulties. One problem with audience studies is that the researcher can dominate their data; they can be in danger of becoming a 'puppeteer', or they can overidentify with 'audience group preferences rather than staying in critical dialogue mode' (Hermes 2012: 198). The role of the researcher in audience studies is a tricky one. You cannot objectify your subjects to the point that they are neutralized, nor can you overempathize with your participants. There is a balancing act between objectivity and subjectivity. Hermes claims 'a hermeneutic approach demands a certain measure of empathy' (ibid.). My approach is to avoid being critical of my participants, but to ask critical questions so that I can understand what is going on. To achieve this I use multiple methods, drawing on quantitative data to gather a wide-ranging perspective on a problem, theory or issue, for example using existing statistics, industry data, surveys with representative samples of audiences. I also use a large amount of qualitative data to gather a focused and detailed perspective on a problem, theory or issue, for example using diaries, interviews, focus groups or participant observation for smaller groups of audience members. This use of different methods allows for multiple perspectives of audiences. 'From the perspective of audience studies, the future offers a real challenge' (ibid.). My challenge is to follow audiences, see their perspectives and feel their experiences in the wider context of culture and society (see Hill 2012 for further information on methods). An appendix contains details of the projects, data sets and audience samples referred to in the book.

AN OVERVIEW OF THE BOOK

As a cultural phenomenon reality TV has a fast and furious history. Although real people have participated in entertainment news, radio and television for a century or more, the history of the reality genre has its roots in 1980s American and British television, and in the rise of infotainment and factual entertainment throughout the 1990s around the world. Chapter 2, Big Brother moment, maps reality TV up to the point of *Big Brother* and the advent of competitive reality formats. This is a story of opportunism in a changing international media market, experimentation in mixed genres and content provision, and representation of ordinary people as popular entertainment. What we shall see from the audience research is that reality TV's successful and controversial mix of fact and fiction came at just the right moment when broadcasting shifted from a traditional model of speaking to its audience, to a niche commercial model of interacting with its audience. This more interactive model of media content in part led to its success as competitive reality where real people coproduced and performed entertainment for television audiences and internet users. However, this success is also one of the reasons for the genre's creative stagnation at the moment. Ratings for reality formats like *Idol* show a downward turn with younger audiences tired of seeing people manufactured as pop idols. Thus, reality TV's innovation as a genre – real people as entertainment – is also its downfall at this historical juncture as the media becomes saturated with people performing themselves.

Chapter 3, Performance of the self, examines the idea of American sociologist Erving Goffman (1959) that life is a multistage drama and we are all performing ourselves. The chapter argues that the dominance of talent shows over the past decade has shifted emphasis from surveillance and governance to ideas of talent, celebrity and performance in reality television. One television executive said (Gary Carter 2013): '[W]e underestimate what a revolution it is to be performing yourself.' Reality formats like *Big Brother* or *Got Talent* make performing yourself centre stage. Producers and participants create high drama and big emotions that can be circulated as 'did you see that!' mediated moments. These big moments become mega moments, repack-aged within highlights of the latest series, or circulated in social media. In its current form there is an intentional manufacturing of performance and our reactions to multiple identities, in every-day conversations and social media gossip. In this way, reacting to performance in reality TV has become a trope within the system. If all we get given in talent formats are big tears, big tantrums, big surprises, then audiences have little room for their own reflections, emotional reactions and moments of surprise.

Chapter 4, Reality TV experiences, explores how the genre is at the forefront of an experience economy where consumer engage-ment, performance and experience are centre stage. From a mar-keting perspective, and the business trends in an experience economy or affective economics, reality TV content draws on narrative, drama and direct experience of life. This mix of fact and fiction helps to create individual and collective cultural experi-ences that people will pay for again and again. Reality talent formats contain tight interactivity in the form of public audi-tions, voting or social media, which function as a driver to increase audience investment in the live event as it builds momentum through the season and is rolled out around the world. Reality television producers and participants work on enhancing drama, tragedy and comedy, rehearsing and scripting certain types of characters and their emotional journey. The 'active style dialogue' of reality performances works alongside vocal and physical performances, creating emotional hubs for audience engagement. Similar to the sports industry, passion play has become a major feature of the genre and its positioning in an experience or emotional economy. Reality TV makes consumers, audiences and publics, contestants and celebrities, visible and audible through participating in shows as live crowds, in audi-tions, as contestants, as themselves, through voting, or making and sharing content for social media, and through gossiping, people watching and public debate. The immersive, interactive elements of reality TV suggest a widening point of consumption for all things social and emotional.

Chapter 5, Reality and sports entertainment, compares two examples of popular culture commonly described as a spectacle of excess. Roland Barthes (1957) wrote that wrestling is a spectacle of excess. Passions are exaggerated and characters display big physical and emotional performances concerning light and dark, fair play and foul play. We can say something similar about reality entertainment, in particular, structured reality and mega formats. Subtlety and ambiguity are not the main attraction of pro wrestling or formatted reality today, instead power play is the name of the game. Empirical research with professional wrestlers, promoters, producers, crowds, audiences, fans and anti-fans allows for an exploration of spectacle, play and passion in these infamous examples of popular culture.

Finally, Chapter 6 concludes by examining the key themes of the book. These themes include the phenomenon of reality TV over the past few decades; the escalation of competitive reality and producer intervention; the ways real people and celebrities perform themselves; audiences, fans and anti-fans; and the spectacle of excess in reality and sports entertainment. The chapter also reflects on the return to authenticity within the genre. For the past 15 years reality television has moved away from the small moments in everyday life to the big moments of tears and tantrums. It has gone so far down the scripted and structured route that there is a hunger once again for the authentic. How authenticity is produced within television creates an interesting dynamic concerning realist aesthetics, for example under-producing a reality series, showing backstage moments, or rough camera work. And there is a dynamic concerning emotional truth within the genre, a search for an authentic or true self in the mediascape. 'The audience's obsession with reality television is about how real people are, how close to their actual self they are being' (Gary Carter 2013). This obsession with performance and authenticity drives developments within the genre and its influence on popular culture.

2

BIG BROTHER MOMENT

They talk about stuff that you talk about.

(12–15-year-old school boy)

Reality television is a relatively new cultural formation. Early examples of entertainment about real people can be found in historical radio and television programmes, where members of the public participated in talk radio or gameshows and light entertainment. But the reality genre we know of today has a fast and furious history. Gary Carter (2013), Chairman of Northern Europe, and Chairman 360° Shine Group, notes: 'As far as genre is concerned, reality TV is the most significant innovation of the last 15 years.' Why has reality TV been such a significant genre over so short a time span?

The genre caught the media industry and popular imagination in the late 1980s as something called infotainment, and gathered pace in the 1990s as something called factual entertainment. In its earlier forms there were a range of programmes such as *999* with reconstructions and public information, *Cops* with 'caught on camera' crime, MTV's *Real World* with fly-on-the-wall observations, or *Animal Hospital* (BBC 1994–2004, UK) with real stories and regular television personalities. These programmes generally offered different kinds of information and entertainment about ordinary people, such as students, hospital workers or pet owners. Then, in the late 1990s, along came *Big Brother, Survivor* and *Pop Idol*. Reality formats took off like rockets. This hybrid form of competitive reality dominated the global media market: not a local series but an international format; not television but cross-media content; not one product but multiple consumption points in media and music, in entertainment and leisure. Anything that contained real people, and celebrities, in some combination of unscripted social observation and competition, became known as reality TV.

Alongside this industry account there also exists the history of audiences for reality TV. What people thought and felt about reality television before and after *Big Brother* is just as much a part of the history of the genre. Intertwined with the institutional players are the individuals, audiences and publics who helped shape its success. According to Carter (2014), 'genre emerges in the dialogue between producer and audience'. Millions of people in diverse cultures and regions were the viewers, fans, users and consumers who turned on the TV, voted, showed up to live events, bought stuff, downloaded videos, tweeted and liked something reality TV had to offer; conversely millions of people, even some of the same people, turned off the TV, refused to vote or participate, bought other stuff, uploaded alternative videos and disliked something about reality TV. Indeed, the more successful reality television became as formatted entertainment during the 2000s, the more it was publicly criticized. This may seem a paradox given the unrivalled success of the genre according to industrial accounts. But the history of reality television audiences is full of opprobrium. This is partly because the genre is populist and tends to attract public censure for being low-brow entertainment for the masses, and partly because some shows cover controversial or taboo subjects in ways that invite censure. Before *Big Brother*, people quietly talked up reality TV and its entertainment about real people – for example this woman said 'it shows you what good television you can make out of absolutely nothing'. After *Big Brother* people talked down reality TV – this man summed it all up as 'really tacky and really kind of sad'.

This chapter maps reality TV up to the point of *Big Brother* and the advent of competitive reality formats. It is a history of two different notions of mediated reality. According to John Corner (2014):

> Earlier forms of Reality TV operated extensively in 'world space', for example cities, shops, police stations, airports, hospitals. Whereas both *Big Brother* and the talent shows operate extensively in 'television space', including variations on the 'studio', or 'studio house'.

The transition from world space to television space around the time of *Big Brother* had important implications for what Corner calls 'reality' relations. It signalled the opportunism of reality TV producers in a changing international media market, where experimentation in mixed genres and content provision generated high ratings and internet users, especially with young audiences. The shift in emphasis from world space in 1990s factual entertainment to the television space of many entertainment formats also signalled changing 'reality' relations in the participation of ordinary people in popular entertainment and audience engagement with these new kinds of celebrities.

The context of America and Britain provide the backdrop to this short history of reality TV. This is because major moments in the development of this entertainment genre arose within the institutional and cultural contexts of America, Britain and Northern Europe. In terms of reality formats Northern Europe, and the UK in particular, took a leading role in format origination, production and distribution, with major formats such as *Strictly Come Dancing* (also *Dancing with the Stars*), *The X Factor*, *Got Talent*, *MasterChef*, *The Voice* and *Big Brother* all originating from format houses based in the UK and Holland. For a global perspective on the history of the genre see edited collections such as *The Reality TV Reader* (Ouellette 2014), *The Politics of Reality Television: Global Perspectives* (Kraidy and Sender 2011), or *Understanding the Global TV Format* (Moran and Malbon 2012) amongst others.

The primary sources of information in this chapter come from people – producers, journalists, audiences. The original data is taken from quantitative surveys, qualitative interviews and household observations during the 1990s and onwards in Britain; the secondary data is taken from news, television content, the internet and other public sources. Despite its popularity, there are still large gaps in empirically led audience research of reality TV. Suffice to say that empirical evidence is the backbone to understanding a history of reality television audiences around the world. For example, whilst *Big Brother* has established itself in the broadcast landscape of America and Britain, it is just beginning in Vietnam (VTV6, 2013–). We can only imagine what an audience study could reveal about the politics and cultural context to the first season of *Big Brother* in such a country.

What we shall see from the audience research is that reality TV's successful and controversial mix of factual entertainment came at just the right moment when broadcasting shifted from a traditional model of speaking to its audience, to a niche commercial model of interacting with its audience. This more interactive model of media content in part led to its success as a genre where real people co-produced and performed entertainment for television audiences and internet users. However, this success is also one of the reasons for the genre's creative stagnation at the moment, as real people become overproduced as entertainment. Thus, reality TV's innovation as a genre – real people as entertainment – is also its downfall at this historical juncture as the media becomes saturated with people performing themselves.

REALITY TV BEFORE *BIG BROTHER*

Imagine watching reality TV in the 1990s. Probably you would have sat in front of a television in the living room or kitchen, with family and friends, and chatted about your day. There would be no social media, no tablets, no catch up on Netflix or BBC iPlayer. There were videos, and people recorded and stored favourite programmes, or timeshifted so they could watch their shows when it suited them, stacking videos the size of books one on top of another around the TV set. There were computers, and a group of early adopters had heavy hard drives and large monitors, connecting to the internet with dial up services, accompanied by a strange high pitched sound and crackling noise reminiscent of a poor radio signal. Still, live television was by far the easiest way to watch shows and in the 1990s television schedulers ruled. Daytime, evening and weekend schedules on broadcast and cable/satellite channels were replete with a wide range of factual entertainment for popular audiences.

The social context for early forms of reality TV was crucial. The majority of broadcast programmes were on once a week during the evening, not stripped over several nights as often happens with contemporary series. Each programme could last for half an hour (*Rescue 911*) or an hour (*America's Most Wanted*, Fox, 1988–2012, USA), including adverts. The coveted weeknight slots promised mass audiences, high ratings and commercial revenues: producers of *America's Most Wanted* could claim over 20 million viewers; in the UK producers of *Airport* (BBC 1996, UK) could boast of a 50 per cent market share (Raphael 1997, 2009; Hill 2005). During this period factual entertainment jostled for position in peak schedules. In the UK programmes were scheduled in the eight o'clock slot, competing with each other on different public service and commercial channels. Factual entertainment slipped easily into people's routines, following on from early evening news bulletins and weekly soap operas. Schedulers knew when to place factual entertainment, as Brunsdon *et al.* (2001) noted the eight o'clock slot was almost a national institution in British broadcasting. Popular factual television, a blend of factual reportage and drama, came at a time when people were winding down after a day at work, putting their children to bed, with half an eye on the TV (Gauntlett and Hill 1999). In a mass observation study of the early 1990s, viewers described the attraction of factual entertainment as something you could tune in and out of whilst going about your everyday routines (Hill 2000b). One woman (aged 18–34) summed it up as 'It's so easy to sit down for half an hour and go "what would I do?"' Perhaps more than anything else, this comment highlights the social attraction of factual entertainment in the 1990s: it was easy to watch and easy to relate to.

Critics of early reality television often claimed it was cheap to make. Chad Raphael (1997; 2009: 129) charted the rise of reality TV as a 'response to the economic restructuring of U.S. television' in the 1980s; big networks were faced with high corporate debt, smaller advertising revenues, and a fragmented audience turning to video and smaller cable and pay-per-view channels. A series of strikes and labour unrest pushed major television producers to use non-union labour and develop unscripted programming along the lines of *Cops* on Fox. Raphael noted how reality TV was 'an integral part of network strategies to control labour unrest' (ibid.). He cited a reality TV producer: 'remember the Writers Guild strike in '88? … That was the year that gave rise to reality TV' (ibid.). Early reality TV was cheap to make and relatively easy to sell abroad, either distributed as an original programme or formatted and remade as a local production in a foreign territory.

In the UK market, similar institutional pressures for cheap, unscripted television led public service and commercial broadcasters to test American and locally made crime and emergency services programming. Despite criticism that this kind of television was sensational tabloid TV, British producers persevered with re-tuning American-style reality into factual entertainment. Changes in media regulation meant that smaller production companies were commissioned to make programmes that were economically viable for the bigger broadcasters. Indeed, just as American reality TV dipped in the mid-1990s, British factual entertainment dominated the market, with independent production houses in the UK and Northern Europe generating new programmes, sub-genres and formats which were tested to great success with the public and then sold to America to be re-made there. As we shall see in the next section, this wave in reality TV led to the creation of entertainment formats, a wildly successful and somewhat more expensive form of media content compared with the early days of *Cops* or *999*.

RANGE OF FACTUAL ENTERTAINMENT

There was a wide range of factual entertainment on offer in the 1990s. For example, an emergency services style of programming followed law enforcement on the job, or doctors in the emergency room, combining facts about professionals and crisis situations with dramatic storylines and identifiable characters. There were programmes involving caught on camera footage. For example car chase style programming like *Police, Camera, Action!*

(ITV 1994–2010, UK) would capture the world's wildest car chases on film and repeatedly show the blurry images from surveillance footage in a moment of dramatic spectacle. Some programmes used a fly-on-the-wall style of filming such as *Driving School* (BBC 1997, UK) where learner drivers were observed trying to get their licence. Also popular in the 1990s were reconstruction programmes like *America's Most Wanted* where criminal acts were re-enacted with a public address for information. And there were early reality formats such as *Changing Rooms* (BBC 1996–2004, UK) where ordinary homes were given a makeover by a team of experts.

The plethora of factual entertainment in the 1990s had historical roots in television, radio, newspapers and magazines. Donald Sassoon in his history of European popular culture said 'culture, all culture, feeds off itself and moves on' (2006: x). This history of reality TV is an example of television cannibalizing itself. The kinds of factual entertainment audiences watched during this decade were feeding off light entertainment and lifestyle from older forms of television. For example there was *Candid Camera* (CBS 1959–67, USA) where the hoax was used as a device to make entertainment from ordinary people and their reactions to created for television situations. Anna McCarthy (2009: 23) used *Candid Camera* as an example of the 'first wave of reality TV'; she looked at the hidden camera as a tool for social knowledge and criticized such depictions of ordinary citizens. The key ingredient of something set up by producers to ensure maximum reactions from people is a feature of many factual entertainment programmes past and present. For McCarthy, *Candid Camera* spawned a 'reality TV generation' (ibid.: 41) where many MTV shows and series like *America's Funniest Home Videos* (ABC 1989–, USA) depict citizens as fools to be laughed at and exploited for entertainment.

Another example includes magazine shows from the seventies such as *Nationwide* (BBC 1969–83, UK) often on in the early evening, where news stories about social issues were interspersed with a makeover feature, perhaps a housewife being given a fashionable new look. News of this kind borrowed heavily from fashion magazines dating back to the early twentieth century, where readers were given a transformation courtesy of make-up and clothing manufacturers (Griffen-Foley 2004). The ingredient of the makeover transformation – the reveal – is another feature of factual entertainment then and now. The influences can be traced in *Changing Rooms*, a popular lifestyle makeover series from the BBC in the nineties where a team of experts rapidly transformed homes into fashionable living spaces. Key to this show was the rather ambitious designers and the reactions of homeowners to their glamorous new living room or bedroom. The moment of the reveal captured the reactions of people, in shock, in tears, happy or angry. The show created a scenario where ordinary people's reactions were captured on camera in the moment of the reveal. This moment was so well known by audiences and participants in the show that people could imitate the facial expressions of people as they reacted in apparent horror or happiness to their new designer rooms. For example, in focus groups with children and young teens in 2000, a group of boys reluctantly admitted to watching *Changing Rooms* with their mum and dad and play acted the moment of the reveal, mimicing the emotional performances of participants. This kind of interplay between producers and audiences illustrates how popular culture feeds off itself.

Factual entertainment borrowed from local television news. For example, some news reportage captured events happening live, using a caught on camera style of address where a news reporter spoke to camera and interviewed people on the street. This mode of address – live in front of the cameras, interspersed with people's reactions – is a recurring feature of factual entertainment. *Cops* was a series where law enforcement officers were filmed on the job, responding to emergency calls and dealing with crime as it happened. Officers were filmed patrolling the streets, arresting drunk and disorderly members of the public, who were interviewed by a film crew as they were put in handcuffs, read their rights, cameras capturing their reactions to an arrest. Officers were also filmed talking to camera, explaining situations, probable scenarios, during and after arrests. Bill Nichols (1994) argued that *Cops* created a narrative that supported law enforcement and promoted a sanitized view of the reality of street crime.

In the 1990s there were a range of programmes using surveillance footage. *Police, Camera, Action!* used footage from fixed cameras attached to law enforcement cars or helicopters showing the spectacle of car chases. In a representative sample of 8,216 respondents, 72 per cent said they liked to watch programmes such as this on a regular and occasional basis; these series were popular with men and women (48 per cent of male respondents, 47 per cent of female respondents), across all ages (50 per cent of 16–34 year olds, 50 per cent of 35–54 year olds), and across social class (50 per cent of upper and upper-middle class, 45 per cent of middle and working class). Audiences enthused about the thrill of the chase and dumb criminals caught on camera. One female viewer (aged 35–50) in 2000 said:

> When I watch some of that *Police, Camera, Action!* and some of the things they do, I just want to shout at them because I can't believe what some of them do, ... that's when you know the programme's good, when you start shouting at your television.

Another kind of surveillance series included the set-up where dodgy builders or mechanics were caught in a sting operation. Sometimes these programmes would be presented by an under-cover journalist with news credentials. This style of factual entertainment was perceived as caught on camera for the public good, championing decency and fairness in an unfair society. As one viewer said: '[T]hat is good, the film is all natural, there ain't no "cut, let's take that again." It's like they've been caught doing wrong and that's it' (male viewer, aged 35–50).

Observational documentaries such as *The American Family* (PBS 1973, USA) or *Sylvania Waters* (ABC 1992, Australia) came from fly-on-the-wall traditions in documentary television. In the early 1990s MTV's *The Real World* borrowed a fly-on-the-wall mode of filming and combined this with a specially created for television social experiment. A group of young people with different personalities and values were brought together for entertainment purposes. Sometimes called reality soap, or more recently known as structured reality, *The Real World* established the importance of casting, storylines, a clash of personalities and wannabe celebrities to the genre. Series such as *Jersey Shore* owe much to MTV's *The Real World*.

British factual entertainment experimented with a hybrid of observational documentary and soap opera genres. *Paddington Green* (BBC 1998–2001, UK), a docusoap about real people living in a London square, was similar to the weekly soap *East-Enders* (BBC 1985–, UK), a fictional account of people living in a London square. Docusoaps were a hit with British audiences. For example two docusoaps *Airport* (BBC 1996–2008, UK) and *Airline* (ITV 1998–2006, UK) were scheduled against each other on the main public service and commercial channels at the same time on the same night. The market became saturated with docusoaps to the point where the public started to tune out: 'I think most of the fly-on-the-wall stuff, most of it's been done to a certain degree. If you want fly-on-the-wall, you've got to find the wall. I mean, they've done this and they've done that, and you say well fair enough' (male viewer, aged 35–50).

PUBLIC AND POPULAR

In terms of the political and institutional contexts to factual entertainment in the 1990s there was an overriding uneasiness about the mix of fact and fiction within the genre as a whole. Academic research addressed the porousity of a hybrid genre that made claims of public service and commercial considerations. Titles such as 'How Real Can You Get?' (Kilborn 1994), signalled the tensions between public and private values within the genre. As Kilborn (2003: 51) noted, changes to the institutional environment in the 1990s 'created exciting opportunities for factual entertainment' and 'sounded the death knell for those more serious forms of documentary work which claimed to be culturally enlightening rather than thinly disguised entertainment vehicles'.

A traditional public service ethos was being eroded within the political and economic climate of the 1990s in America and Britain. The political agenda during the Reagan and Thatcher years of the 1980s ensured that some of the leading ideas of neoliberal politics, such as free individuals unheeded by state intervention, were permeating public service and commercial broadcasting. Despite differences within neoliberal politics and television markets in America and Britain, some similar political and institutional factors were behind the drive in factual entertainment. Public service broadcasting, like other welfare state formations, was under attack. Commercial and niche channels gained ground. As a genre experiment, factual entertainment packaged an uneasy mix of public service and commercial imperatives.

Chad Raphael (1997) in his study of the political economics of 'reali-TV' in America pointed out the promotion of traditional public service credentials to highlight the civic value of shows like *America's Most Wanted*. Producers claimed that according to the *FBI Law Enforcement Bulletin* the series 'organised some 22 million viewers into the first neighbourhood watch association' (Nelson 1989: 5, cited in Raphael 1997, 2009: 133). In Britain, the BBC was criticized for producing factual entertainment as a means to garner mass audiences and high ratings. Producers claimed that shows like *999* were much more public service than the American version *Rescue 911* (see Hill 2000a). Kilborn noted 'a due measure of public service gravitas' in the documentary-style narrative of behind the scenes at the emergency services, or the news presenter as anchor to the programme, and at the same time a great attention to dramatic re-enactments (2003: 72). One producer said they eschewed documentary techniques in favour of drama 'as a way of making factual television more accessible to a big audience' (Powell *et al.* 1992: 32, cited in Kilborn 2003: 72).

Audience research at the time indicated that British viewers performed the work of finding civic values in entertainment vehicles. In a representative sample of 8,216 respondents in 2000, 54 per cent liked to watch hospital and emergency services series such as *999*. These series were popular with men and women (33 per cent of male respondents, 37 per cent of female respondents), across all ages (37 per cent of 16–34 year olds, 35 per cent of 35–54 year olds), and across social class (35 per cent of upper and upper-middle class, 36 per cent of middle and working class). For example, this description of *999* illustrated the perception of public good within factual entertainment in the 1990s:

> I thought these programmes demonstrated the very BEST of human behaviour and endeavour. All programmes gave the viewer a 'buzz' – that oh so rare feeling you can get from a really gripping drama.

> I think 999 serves a useful purpose in reassuring viewers that there are LARGE numbers of people in society committed to working on behalf of others. An antidote to incessant shock/horror news broadcasts.
>
> (56-year-old male, single parent)

This viewer used the tactic of counterposing a sensational trend in tabloid news journalism against a more 'useful' public service endeavour of *999*, a programme about people who save lives. A public service gravitas permeates their comments about a commercial enterprise.

In another example from the early 1990s, a British viewer commented on the docusoap *Children's Hospital* (BBC 1993–2002, UK):

> When I am watching their cases I feel like crying for them and their families and all the staff who are doing their best to ease the suffering. After watching I feel really humble. These children and families are going through so much and it makes you realize how lucky you are to be healthy.
>
> (23-year-old female student)

Like most viewers of this docusoap about children battling acute illness, this woman was aware of criticism in the press, and by the public, that people who watched this series were taking pleasure from other people's pain. Kilborn noted the term 'ghoul TV' for these kinds of shows (2003: 62). 'I feel really humble' is a tactic to counteract such widespread criticism.

The public–private issue that dominated factual entertainment throughout the 1990s was overshadowed at the end of the decade by the development of competitive reality and the international success of formats like *Survivor* and *Big Brother*. These reality formats did not spring from nowhere. They were the result of a series of transformations within the media industries and genre experimentations throughout the mid- to late 1990s. Certain producers of factual entertainment were at the forefront of a sea change in broadcasting. These producers understood that audiences, especially younger viewers, liked the mixed messages of public and popular. They were hungry for a different type of television that engaged them in dialogue rather than spoke to them as teacher to student.

Gary Carter (2013) commented:

> Up until the mid nineties television had been modernist in the sense that it was doing that Reithian thing of informing, educating and entertaining the public. It assumed a power dynamic. We who know better – usually men – are telling you what is happening in the world. And we control the means of production and therefore we control the argument. By the time I joined Planet 24 young people were questioning the mainstream ideal. There was a different kind of power dynamic. It was a riff on the conventions of this modernist television, shifting from modern to postmodern television.

The political and industrial contexts to the 1990s in Britain provided fertile ground for a transformation from modern to postmodern media. Carter explains:

> This is connected to the rise of commercial television and the fragmentation of television into servicing niches. When *Survivor* arose out of that company, Planet 24 … we consciously merged genres. What happens if we take a documentary and push it together with a talk show and we jam it into a gameshow?

What took producers of early reality TV by surprise was the instant appeal of something like *Survivor*. The innovation in genre experimentation coupled with the display of ordinary people doing mundane things was a revelation. It was a different power dynamic. One viewer compared the mode of address in public service broadcasting as akin to having dinner with your grandparents (Hill 2007). No wonder audiences responded to competitive reality with such zeal: viewers were being invited to a big and noisy event, not a quiet dinner with grandpa.

The story of *Castaway* exemplifies the change from what Carter describes as modernist to postmodernist television. *Castaway* (BBC 2000, UK) was a year-long documentary shown on the BBC around the same time in the year 2000 as *Big Brother* in Britain (there was also a second season in the mid-2000s).

Executive producer Jeremy Mills from Lion Television had a public service background and a tradition in observational documentary television. The premise was to send a group of volunteers (men, women, families, singles) to a remote Scottish island to live for a year away from everyday routines and creature comforts. A film crew documented their experiences and every few months a programme was shown on BBC depicting life on the island. In a representative survey of 8,216 adult respondents aged 16–65+ (UK 2000), 38 per cent watched the series on a regular/occasional basis, and 51 per cent never saw it. For younger viewers, aged 4–15 (unweighted sample 937, UK 2000), 33 per cent were regular/occasional viewers, and 58 per cent never saw it. Of those that watched the series, the majority were aged 13–15 and 16–34 (around one-third of the samples). There was no discernable difference in gender or social class for these viewing profiles, except younger viewers were more likely to be in the upper and upper-middle class, perhaps reflecting parental viewing preferences.

The following quotes highlighted how audiences responded to *Castaway* at the time:

> I was just amazed that people would want to do that and just wanted to see their progress to see how they coped with it.
>
> (18–34-year-old female viewer)

> *Castaway* that is the one that is just something from nothing, you've never had that experience ... and that really has caught the whole family ... You know, you need a lot of courage to do that ... I'm looking forward to the next part of *Castaway* to see what they've done, because each time they've done so much.
>
> (35–50-year-old male viewer)

> On *Castaway* they've got to stay there for a year. ... It goes on so long, it's like you can see how they start off really like 'oh what will we do, what will we do?!' But then like half a year later they've all worked out and they're living properly. And if they have a problem, they've got weeks to sort it out.
>
> (12–15-year-old schoolboy)

Viewers repeatedly referred to the courage of participants in *Castaway*; these were people who carried themselves with dignity under difficult conditions, a keep-calm-and-carry-on attitude that audiences aspired to themselves.

The timing of *Castaway* was its downfall. It should have been a triumph of popular factual and civic values. It started out with ratings of around nine million, but over the year public interest declined. According to BBC News, in a year of reality TV 'all that marks the castaways out is that they are the only people who have not heard of *Big Brother*' (Gallagher 2000). A hybrid public service and commercial broadcaster, Channel 4 had tested the water with *Shipwrecked* (Channel 4 2000–2009, UK), where young people on a warm desert island were forced to live together. The series was a light social experiment. This young male viewer (aged 12–15) noted: 'It was alright, it was a bit commercial, like they always gave them rice, they didn't actually hunt for their food or anything ... They were allowed to go to the shops, which is stupid.' The broadcaster bought *Big Brother*, after a successful first run in Holland. This format was a social experiment like *Shipwrecked*. It had mainly young participants like MTV's *The Real World*; and people were locked into living together like *Castaway*. What was different? *Big Brother* had elimination, public voting, cross-platform content and stripped scheduling.

For Carter, *Big Brother* took the riff on modernist television to the next level with a genre and production experiment (2013):

> Traditionally, television – like film – is produced by taping or filming as little as possible, because of the expense of doing so. But by the mid-90s digital technology allowed you to capture as much as possible, and as soon as you can do that you can make – or edit – many versions of the same story, and this is truly postmodern television. It has no stable point of view. The material is the same, but the reception is different.

In the history of reality TV *Castaway* was overshadowed by competitive reality. The next section looks at the reception of the *Big Brother* moment that changed the face of television, turning it into a billion-dollar game (Bazalgette 2005).

THE BIG BROTHER MOMENT

Big Brother is a major development of reality TV as a global entertainment genre. Formats consultant Julie Donovan noted: '[T]he term reality TV came into my world with the launch of *Big Brother*. I don't think reality TV was even a phrase people could explain before *Big Brother*' (Donovan 2013). What is so special about this show that it would become a defining feature of the genre itself? In retrospect, there were a number of factors that made *Big Brother* a force to be reckoned with. Some of the institutional and political-economic issues were discussed in the previous section. From the point of view of *Big Brother* audiences there were three key factors: it was a staged event; it showed ordinary people being themselves; and these people were in a competitive entertainment format.

STAGED EVENT

Kilborn's book *Staging the Real* (2003: 83) signalled the development of *Big Brother* as a format that overtly referred to reality as 'quite literally being staged'. The genre experiment of observational documentary, gameshow, soap opera and sporting event, is conducted in a 'highly knowing manner', keying into 'audiences' generic knowledge of a wide range of television practices' (Kilborn 2003: 82). This postmodern riff on reality TV was to become part and parcel of the genre, where producers and audiences knowingly jammed fact and fiction together. The advent of *Big Brother* marked the moment when entertainment, drama and performance took centre stage: the term reality TV fooled no one.

Big Brother was a stripped event on a national scale. The first seasons in countries such as the Netherlands, Britain, Sweden, Finland, Australia and America signalled the advent of a major annual reality event promoted across television, newspapers, radio and the internet. Moran and Malbon call *Big Brother* a mega format (2012). Few could resist the draw of the first series. People who refused to watch it took an oppositional stand, giving rise to an entirely new generation of reality refusniks (Hill 2007). For example, this male viewer (aged 18–34) said, 'I chose myself not to watch it because the whole of the universe was watching it and it was getting on my nerves.' One female viewer (aged 18–34) explained:

> I absolutely hated Big Brother ... I can't see the attraction to it. I don't find anything appealing about watching it. It was the same sort of thing every episode, you know. And sometimes you watched it and it was just a room with two people sitting in a chair and you think, what?!

These anti-fans would grow in numbers as *Big Brother* became a regular reality event. Reality refusniks included vocal public figures, TV critics, politicians, news journalists and viewers who had reached their limit of factual entertainment flooding the evening television schedules. Sir Peter Bazalgette was the executive producer at Endemol when the format was launched in the UK. He was described by the *Daily Mail* newspaper in 2013 'as the man who brought us the vulgar beast that is *Big Brother* and who, more than any other television executive, stands accused of turning reality television into staple fodder for the masses' (Johnson 2013). One Labour MP said Bazalgette had 'dumbed down, trivialised and sexualised mass TV viewing' (ibid.).

A passionate relationship with the show was similar to sporting fans and highlighted the live event status and followers of particular contestants in the house. There were fans and anti-fans of contestants and also the entire show. For the first season, *Big Brother* became something of a national sport in Britain. Helped by tabloid newspapers and celebrity gossip magazines, the show was the talking point of the summer of 2000. Douglas Wood, Head of Audience Research at Shine Group, was working at Channel 4 for the first season of *Big Brother*. He said: '[S]omething came along and changed. You felt like you were part of something and what you did during the day carried on with your friends at night and on television and live streaming' (2013).

Participants in focus groups would introduce themselves as *Big Brother* addicts. For example, this woman (aged 18–34) introduced herself to the group as: 'I'm addicted to *Big Brother* and so was my eight-year-old daughter. And it was a bit of a nightmare because she wouldn't go to bed till it finished [laughs].' Many self-confessed addicts were apologetic, as they expected other people to be judgemental of their *Big Brother* addiction. One female viewer (aged 18–34) explained: 'I don't know, I thought it was actually rubbish that programme but I was so hooked I had to keep watching it!' Part of this apologetic viewing was related to the low status of reality TV, but it also connected with traditional modes of engagement for soap opera. As *Big Brother* borrowed from the soap genre in its characterization and interwoven storylines, it also generated gossipy viewing environments of the kind noted by other researchers of soap audiences (see Hobson 2003, Allen 1985, amongst others).

If the show was an addiction then it was one viewers often tried to downplay. In a representative survey of 8,216 respondents in 2000, 54 per cent said they never watched programmes like *Big Brother*. This included 59 per cent men, 50 per cent women; 35 per cent aged 16–34, compared with 64 per cent 55+; 55 per cent upper to upper-middle class, and 54 per cent middle to lower class. Only 12 per cent of respondents claimed to regularly watch real people programmes like *Big Brother*, and 22 per cent occasionally watched. Of the occasional viewers 21 per cent were men and 23 per cent women. There was an age difference for regular viewers, with around 30 per cent of younger viewers, aged 16–34, compared with older viewers of around 15 per cent aged 55 and over; there was little difference according to social class, with around 25 per cent of upper- and upper-middle-class viewers, and 20 per cent of middle- and working-class viewers.

Compared with the ratings for the first season, it was likely respondents downplayed their viewing patterns. The first season finale attracted around ten million viewers, and over seven million phone calls. In a study of television and everyday life in the 1990s one of the findings was that more men watched soaps, but felt guilty about admitting it (Gauntlett and Hill 1999). These female viewers (aged 18–34) of *Big Brother* noted:

Sandra: They [men] always say they're not interested but they do sit down and watch it!
General: Yeah!

Chris: You're at work and you're all girls talking together about *Big Brother* and, all of a sudden, the men join in. They sit there very quietly at first and you say something that clearly hits their trigger and it's like 'Oh yeah, when he said ... !' And it's like 'right, right'!

For younger viewers, children, teenagers and the all important 16–34-year-old target audience, there was a more open acknowledgement of watching *Big Brother*. In a representative survey of 937 respondents aged 4–15 (unweighted sample, 2000, UK), 51 per cent were regular/occasional viewers of programmes like *Big Brother*; 32 per cent were regular viewers, 30 per cent males, 34 per cent females, with the majority aged 10–15 years (around half of the sample), and upper and upper-middle class (39 per cent) compared with middle to working class (27 per cent).

A group of young boys (aged 12–15) explained what they liked about the gossipy side of *Big Brother* in Britain:

Martin: It was sort of the cliffhanger cos every week they were saying like 'oh, who's going to get voted out?' and stuff so you had to keep watching.

Jack: When it got really emotional when there was like arguments. And they talk about stuff that you talk about.

Shaun: And they act the way you'd act. And like the bitching that's going on in the house, it's almost like school.

This is a good example of what John Corner (2002) described as nosey sociability. These viewers responded to the soap opera elements, such as the cliffhanger of the weekly eviction, and the dramatic elements such as the emotional performances in the house. But also, viewers responded to watching real people be themselves (see Chapter 3 on performance). This riff on reality was crucial to the *Big Brother* attraction, the soap opera brought the performance of the self to life – 'they talk about stuff you talk about' and 'they act the way you'd act'.

In its early incarnation *Big Brother* was a staged reality event. Endemol referred to it as a real-life soap. Fictional genres such as soap opera or melodrama were mixed with entertainment genres such as gameshows, and sporting genres such as the live competitive event; and the realist aesthetics knowingly referred to the television and internet surveillance of contestants who were in the early days relatively unaware of what was going on outside the house. These two schoolboys (aged 12–15) summed up their view of the *Big Brother* phenomenon:

> Mark: Can I just say, I think the great thing about *Big Brother* and the reason so many people watched it, is because it's like no other programmes actually show real people, erm ... like programmes like *EastEnders* are completely acted but no other programme has filmed the whole of someone's life.
>
> Mike: Yeah and also in *Big Brother* ... they were completely showing themselves the whole time but on the internet they showed them having number twos!

The genre experiment of staged reality produced 'did you see that!' moments and this was to set a precedent for much reality TV in the following decade.

ORDINARY PEOPLE

The first seasons of *Big Brother* featured ordinary people. Gary Carter (2013) reflected on the early days of the show:

> Real people were like astronauts on the moon. We had never seen them before. They had no expectations and we had no expectations ... they are that rarest of all mythological beasts as far as television is concerned – they are real people.

In *Big Brother* there were a group of diverse personalities all thrown together in a closed artificial environment with cameras everywhere, even in the shower. People like this were part of everyday life, but it was novel to have cameras follow their every move in a TV show. They made a cup of tea, you made a cup of tea. Something so mundane was made utterly strange. It was like watching someone walk on the moon – you saw the world differently.

Perhaps one of the most common references to *Big Brother* in that first season was the novelty of watching someone sleep. Gary Carter (2013) noted:

> What surprised us was the degree to which the audience went for it. They had never seen themselves like this before. I remember my mother who was seventy and who had pooh poohed every description of *Big Brother* I had given her, saying to me 'I am watching these people sleep!'

Douglas Wood (2013) also commented: '[Y]ou actively chose to watch these people when they were sleeping. It's very hard to rationalise this and ask yourself why am I actually enjoying watching someone sleep?' *Guardian* TV critic Stuart Heritage (2013a) reflected on the novelty of watching people sleep:

> I once watched an episode of *Big Brother* where nothing happened. It was live, it was Sunday afternoon and all the housemates were napping in the garden, so nothing happened. Maybe one of them would scratch their nose or roll over, but that was it. It was an hour of sleeping, sound tracked by the distant buzz of planes overhead. And, even though it's obviously massively creepy to say that you enjoy watching people sleep, I could have watched it for much longer. In a very gentle way, it was just as exciting and disruptive as anything else I've seen.

The ordinariness of people, snoozing in the garden, or making a cup of tea, is a disruptive idea for television. Normally television programmes try to grab your attention, and then keep it for as long as possible. Commercial television needs audience attention to satisfy its advertisers, and public service television needs audiences to justify a public licence fee. In the world of art, performance artists have explored people sleeping, eating, sometimes having sex, and this is part of an exposition that the mundane can be interesting, even political. Popular television is not an obvious platform for radical statements about the mundane.

A group of teenage girls (aged 12 to 15) explained what was so compelling about the first season of *Big Brother* in Britain:

Laura: On most TV programmes like all the other ones, they show a family where they're all like loving and everything. *Big Brother* just shows the normal side, cos that's how people act in real life ...

Maria: I just thought it was boring cos I didn't care about any of the people. It was really slow. The storyline wasn't fast moving, it was just boring. I wouldn't choose to watch that.

Fay: Yeah, but if you'd watched it all the way through, then you'd know the people and you'd know they'd been doing it for a long time and you're like waiting for them to do it, to finally get up to it ...

Emily: You can go behind people's backs basically. And there's no storyline to it. It's like there's no storyline, anything can happen.

Joanna: It just goes along naturally.

This was an example of how viewers saw the mundane as strange in the first season. People are boring in real life; 'it just goes along naturally'. Without a clear storyline, there's a slow burn, waiting, watching, knowing; 'anything can happen'.

The innovation of this genre experiment was that the cameras caught the mundane nature of living in a confined space where small things became interesting. The girls in the discussion above were talking about the backstabbing that became part of the first season of the series. One of the contestants, nicknamed Nasty Nick by the tabloid papers, had been trying to influence voting behaviour. These young viewers described how they had been waiting for him to be found out by the other contestants. The 24-hour surveillance had given viewers at home privileged knowledge of Nasty Nick. One of the girls described how this insider view, a classic fly-on-the-wall technique from observational documentary, made the mundane much more interesting:

> Maria: In real life you can't always see what someone's talking about or they're thinking. In *Big Brother* you always see different things go on which you wouldn't usually see in day-to-day life ... say if you run off and cry and no one knew about it, you'd see it on *Big Brother*.

Thus, the show offered viewers the chance to see the boring routine of day-to-day life and an all-knowing perspective on the contestants' lives within the show.

The combination of ordinary people being themselves and their every private move being caught on camera created an odd narrative of people becoming characters in front of the viewing public. As this was in real time, the slow transformation from person, to contestant, to television personality took place day by day with the cooperation of the producers and viewers. Kavka and West called this real-time moment 'a coincidence of experience between viewers and participants' (2004: 151). The girls who argued about the mundanity of *Big Brother* also recognized the process of characterization within the premise of the show.

> Laura: Well, I think there's got to be a bad person in TV programmes.
> Fay: It's just how they get on and the way you relate to it really.
> Emily: Well, erm, what I got from people at school was that it wasn't for the informative part or anything it was just basically bitching about other people, they were just like 'I don't like him, I don't like her, I think he should win ... ' That was all basically it was. It was just entertainment.

For the girls who liked the show, the process of characterization was one of its key attractions, where viewers related with the people turned contestants, voting out characters they disliked and rooting for favourites. For those who disliked the show, the bitching and backstabbing became a means to criticize the series. Perjorative terms like 'it's just entertainment' quickly became common in everyday chatter about *Big Brother*.

The speed with which people distanced themselves from their early love affair with *Big Brother* signals both a strength and weakness of the premise of the show. Once ordinary people transformed from contestants to television personalities there was no going back to the early novelty of the moment when you caught yourself watching people sleeping. Douglas Wood (2013) explained:

> This is related to the fall of reality TV, people falling out of love with it. That first season of *Big Brother*, the contestants were so unselfaware. They didn't really fully understand what they were doing either. It felt natural and authentic and you didn't feel that slightly cynical manipulation that you felt in later reality series where contestants were so self aware, consciously self editing. There was something genuinely fresh in the first season, with people who had interesting stories to tell. That had not been done before.

Two recent trends in television have tried to recapture that first sense of excitement in watching people do nothing much at all. Slow TV is a Norwegian television trend where you can watch a fire burning, or someone knitting for hours at a time. Similar to muzak, it is about creating an atmosphere rather than directing specific reactions. *Gogglebox* (Channel 4 2013–, UK) is another trend, watching people watch TV. TV critic Grace Dent (2013) wrote: 'There's something rather joyous and soothing about *Gogglebox*. It reminds me a touch of series one *Big Brother* when participants were in the main reserved, unaffected and compellingly natural.' The next section considers the transition from unaffected to self-aware contestants in this reality format.

REAL PEOPLE AS ENTERTAINMENT

The format of *Big Brother* put real people into a competitive environment. The competition element comes from the gameshow experiment, where contestants participate in a game with a cash prize, and also sporting events, where amateurs participate in a live elimination. Real people were always a feature of gameshows and reality TV, but *Big Brother* shifted the emphasis to the elimination of real people by the public. The catchphrase 'You decide' helped bring the point home to viewers and internet users who phoned, texted and voted in their millions. Douglas Wood (2013) noted: 'people stopped being normal and became characters fundamental to the entertainment process.'

Gary Carter (2013) commented:

> To begin with, we had never seen people like this, in this way, before – and they were prepared to do it, to compete and to be at the same time. Then, the form started to exploit the audience's belief that the inhabitants' motivation was media exposure and real world exploitation, regardless of whether fame or money come to the inhabitants in the long term.

Two male viewers (aged 18–34) reflected on the motivations for competing in *Big Brother* after the first season in Britain:

Daniel: The thing is when you're being filmed, I think probably your attitude might change a bit, you're not going to be yourself ...

Colin: They've got to make you worth watching, aint they.

Here, then, an essential component of *Big Brother*, people competing and being at the same time, becomes a problem of exploitation where producers and contestants have 'got to make you worth watching'.

One example of ordinary people competing and being at the same time is that of a female contestant Mel, who appeared in the first season of *Big Brother* in Britain. She was a source of gossip as viewers disliked her double act of being herself and playing the game. These female viewers (aged 18–34) talked about her performance:

Lisa: I don't think she ever forgot that the cameras were there ...

General: No, no.

Lisa: ... she was plucking her pubic hairs with her tweezers!

Angela: Oh my god!

Lisa: In the garden with everyone else watching!

General: [comment and laughter]

Bev: You can just tell that she loved herself, she always had to look immaculate, she paid too much attention to her appearance ...

Fiona: And there are times when you don't want to be nice to people in normal life and you don't want to look lovely ... but she was too good to be true, I think.

Bev: But, it looked false a lot of it.

Fiona: Yeah, that's what I mean.

Bev: She was jumping from one man to the next, wasn't she?

Fiona: As one was voted out, she went to somebody else didn't she?

Sue: No one's that nice ...

Fiona: No, that's what I'm trying to say.

Bev: She loved herself too much.

Attitudes towards contestants shifted to negative criticism of their personalities and motivations. Indeed the premise of *Big Brother*, ordinary people competing, starts to become suspect and suspicion sinks into audience attitudes and beliefs.

Gary Carter (2013) describes the shift in attitudes towards ordinary people as contestants as a double escalation:

> First of all, future contestants start to base their behaviour on what they have seen and they believe is the strategy for success in these competitive shows, to escalate the quality of their personal performances so they become weirder and weirder. They think they have to behave in more and more outrageous ways. And the producers can't quite believe that the series is as interesting if they don't intervene. So they intervene in casting and the kinds of people who are applying.

Audiences quickly caught on: 'you're supposed to think "well, that's how people are". But they're not; you're getting these extreme personalities in a forced environment just creating something that is really weird' (30-year-old female bar manager).

Big Brother started out as something exciting and different, with contestants compellingly natural in unnatural settings. This freshness and innocence – I'm watching someone sleep! – could not last. In a short space of time the format became a platform for real people to perform an extreme version of themselves and the public became wise to this game. The double escalation of producers and contestants intervening in *Big Brother* set reality TV off in another direction over the coming decade. Competitive reality and global formats such *The X Factor* became juggernauts of primetime television and cross-media. Looking back on the *Big Brother* moment we can say that competitive reality formats disrupted the development of the genre, taking reality in another direction. Julie Donovan (2013) noted: '*Big Brother* has become inauthentic. You cannot get the innocence back.'

CONCLUSION

A history of reality TV has to take into account audiences. This statement does not deny the significance of producers who literally put reality TV together; or broadcasters and network executives who commission and schedule reality TV series; nor institutional and political players who create policies and regulations that provide fertile ground for reality entertainment. The deregulation of media ownership and the burgeoning of niche channels for fragmented audiences led the way for international, commercial factual entertainment. Certainly, reality TV gained momentum in the 1990s as an entertainment genre that was in tune with fundamental institutional changes. This opportunistic genre was the cultural form of choice for producers who wanted to shift from broadcast television that speaks to its audience, to commercial television and multimedia that interacts with its audience. All of these points serve to underscore how well reality TV works as a mixed generic form within a global entertainment industry. But no genre can exist without audiences. As Steve Neale notes, genre is multidimensional (1980). It has been the task of this chapter to allow audiences to speak alongside other political, economic or production matters. People are a significant dimension of the development of reality TV because they have both watched and participated in it. Whether in the form of infotainment, factual entertainment or the reality TV we know of today, audiences, contestants and participants have been alert to the riff on reality within the genre.

Nowhere is this riff on reality more apparent to audiences than in the rise of competitive reality. *Big Brother* is a competitive reality format that marks a major moment in the history of this entertainment genre. Just as a history of reality TV has to take into account audiences, so too does it need to do justice to this seismic shift in the reality television landscape. As one producer noted, no one really knew what reality TV was before *Big Brother*. This format took previous elements from earlier programmes, such as people forced together in a confined space, or caught on camera and surveillance footage, and introduced stripped scheduling, competition, public voting and multimedia to the mix. The result was an innovative show that everyone was talking about. Audiences knew *Big Brother* was staged; they referred to it as similar to a soap opera, or as one young viewer noted, it was a bit like being at school. And at the same time there was something compellingly natural about the ordinary people who were part of this show. The freshness of the *Big Brother* format quickly gave way to an exploitation of ordinary people as contestants, where people began to perform extreme versions of themselves. This knowing self-awareness was to be the hallmark of competitive reality that has come to dominate entertainment since the 2000s.

The riff on reality that marked the moment of *Big Brother* became more forceful and artificial after the international success of competitive reality formats. Later seasons showed contestants and producers escalating the performance of ordinary people to such an extent that audiences lost their belief in any playful claims to reality in the genre. After *Big Brother*, the premise of reality became suspect. A TV reviewer in 2009 marked the end of *Big Brother* in Britain as 'the coming of age of reality TV, and more specifically its audience. Not in a good way, obviously ... reality, as in the genre, has made extraordinary incursions into reality, as in the place we all live' (Hyde 2009). Already in 2003 audiences were aware of incursions into reality. As this viewer reflected: '*Big Brother* was a new thing, but then, I don't know, reality TV ... it's not even reality anymore. It's completely emptied and made. Somebody else is making some reality for us' (43-year-old unemployed male).

3

PERFORMANCE OF THE SELF

I just think that's life cos at the end of the day everyone lies.
(15-year-old schoolgirl)

There is a play-off between performance and authenticity in reality TV. 'Everyone wore masks these days, and they seldom slipped. The extreme was the reality-based television shows, where people created meta versions of themselves by trying to act in a way they thought was natural' (Lippman 2000: 176). Such a comment in the novel *The Sugar House* highlights how we should never takes things at face value. We all perform ourselves to some degree, putting on a mask to hide the 'real me' from the world at large. Reality television represents the extreme form of this everyday role-playing, a mediated space for a 'meta me'.

American sociologist Erving Goffman wrote a key book in 1959 called *The Presentation of the Self in Everyday Life*. Perhaps this book, more than any other academic study, is a meta-text for reality television. Goffman's concept is that we perform ourselves in multiple ways, living life as part of a social drama. To make a connection between Goffman and reality TV is not new. From the early days of research in this genre, scholars have highlighted the ways reality TV captures on camera the banality of everyday life and the ways audiences engage with the individual and collective performances of people caught on camera (see Corner 2002, Kilborn 2003 amongst others). This performative and entertainment frame can be sidelined in discussions of surveillance and reality TV. This chapter argues that the dominance of talent shows over the past decade has shifted emphasis from surveillance and governance to ideas of talent, celebrity and performance. It should be said that reality TV can be about both surveillance and performance (McGrath 2004). However, the focus on audience engagement with competitive reality formats in this chapter lends itself to reflections on performance, following other audience research along the lines of Beverly Skeggs and Helen Wood (2012) on performance and personhood, or Laura Grindstaff (2011) on celebrity and performance in everyday life.

John Corner (2009: 62) cautions that Goffman's idea of routine performance is not to be lifted wholesale to reality television. There are differences between performing yourself in the kitchen and in front of a camera crew with an expected audience of millions. But, it is a testament to Goffman's original idea that the performance of the self becomes increasingly relevant to the development of reality TV within the media matrix (Meyrowitz 1985). Our sense of self, performance mode and the reactions of others may be different, but there is a connection. It has become a cliché now that performers in talent shows refer to themselves as former audiences – 'I was a big fan, and now I can't believe I'm here in the studio'. The 2013 series of *Strictly Come Dancing* (BBC1, UK) showcased a superfan – from sofa to sequinned ball gown. The double identity of audience and performer connects with the internet where YouTube videos of auditions can garner more attention than televized screenings. For example, the Susan Boyle audition of 'I dreamed a dream' on *Britain's Got Talent* (ITV1, UK) has over 300 million hits on YouTube. Highly performative and emotional moments in reality TV are a feature of many formats, filmed in bite-sized form for commercial television and social media.

Gary Carter, Chairman of Northern Europe, Chairman of 360° Shine Group, notes (2013): '[W]e underestimate what a revolution it is to be performing yourself.' He explains: '[T]he revolutionary nature of this performance is because reality television allowed the individual participant to move from being the subject of the argument of another (typically, the film maker) to being the generator of the argument' (Carter 2014). Reality formats like *Big Brother* (Endemol) in the early 2000s or *Pop Idol* (19 and FremantleMedia) today make performing versions of yourself centre stage. 'For example, *Big Brother* requires a performance as "national everyperson", while *Idol* requires a performance of "me as pop idol"' (Carter 2014). Producers and participants create high drama and big emotions that can be circulated as 'did you see that!' mediated moments. These big moments – a tearful audition in *American Idol* (Fox, USA), a broken shoulder on the ice rink in *Dancing on Ice* (ITV1, UK) – become mega moments, repackaged within high-lights of the latest series, or circulated in social media. In turn, audiences talk about performance, multiple identities, and notions of truth and artifice, in everyday conversations and social media gossip. One young viewer succinctly described the performance of the self in reality TV as: 'I just think that's life cos at the end of the day everyone lies' (15-year-old schoolgirl). The fact that reality TV invites commentary on the notion 'everyone lies' in a strange way opens a door to reflection on the multiple realities of the world we live in.

PERFORMANCE

The idea of performance is multifaceted. In its most literal form as audience–performer interaction for live theatre it can mean the live performance of a theatre production, for example if you are in Leicester Square, London there are advertisements for tickets to a theatre show. Performance in this sense means the production of a show whereby a collective group is responsible for an overall performance, typically a production company with a director, producer, scriptwriter, set designer, camera, lighting and sound operators, actors or participants, amongst others. Then, there is the performance of an individual playing a role, for example critics singled out the performance of an actor in *I Can't Sing!*, a musical based on the television series *The X Factor*. Performance in this sense means one person's ability to play a role or showcase a talent, drawing on various skills and experience to produce a vocal, physical, musical and/or emotional performance.

It is worth making a distinction between acting by a performer and the production of a performance, as these practices are somewhat different. An individual usually works with other actors, dancers or musicians, and industry professionals to collectively construct a performance. Still, an individual performer can be singled out for their part, winning an award for best actor in a new musical, for example. The production of a performance is often judged on the work of people front and back stage who deliver a successful show. There are certain professionals who claim more of the spotlight than others. The comedian Harry Hill was co-writer of *I Can't Sing!* and part of the publicity for the production; when *I Can't Sing!* closed after less than two months at the London Palladium it was Harry Hill's name that was cited in the press. Still, this satirical musical did not fail because of one person, but relied on the collective production of the show and the willingness of the theatre public to pay to see a live performance.

The performance modes of reality TV are multifaceted in the sense that traditionally distinct groups of creative producers, participants/performers and audiences become interconnected. Whilst there is some overlap between individual performers and the collective production of *I Can't Sing!*, there are still distinctions between the actor playing the part of Simon Cowell, or the writer of the lines the actor is speaking or singing in that role. The actors and writers co-create the performance together, following working practices within the profession. However, there are not such clear working practices for the ordinary people who audition for *The X Factor*: they are not all actors who are members of a professional union such as Equity and yet they do sign consent forms to appear in a televized production; they are not all given a script to read and yet they do play an established role in a talent show audition, a role familiar to them from watching previous shows.

The idea of performance that is the basis of this research on audiences extends the notion of performer–audience interaction in theatre to everyday life. Richard Schechner (1977, 2004: 22) wrote that 'performance is a "quality" that can occur in any situation rather than a fenced off genre'. Victor Turner (1986) developed an anthropology of performance, an approach that addressed the relations between the performer and audience as a process of transformation for a group and an individual. Abercrombie and Longhurst (1998: 38) argue:

> Critical to what it means to be a member of an audience is the idea of performance. Audiences are groups of people before whom a performance of one kind or another takes place. Performance, in turn, is an activity in which the person accentuates his or her behaviour under the scrutiny of others.

They argue for an understanding of cultural performance that builds on the work of Schechner and Turner, looking at different performance modes (1998: 43) in public and private spaces, local and global contexts, and in particular in mediascapes, something they call mediatized performance (ibid.).

To add to this broad understanding of cultural or mediatized performance, is the work of Erving Goffman and his idea of the performance of the self (1959). People have a front-stage self they knowingly perform for audiences, and they have a back-stage self that offers a more authentic, or true, version of the self. Goffman contends that people use props, or resources, from everyday life to help in the performance of the self. And as people gather these props, they construct performances of the self that showcase public and private personas. For Goffman, social interaction is about a face-to-face encounter, and a performance 'may be defined as all the activity of [a] given participant on a given occasion which serves to influence in any way any of the other participants' (1959: 26). Performance is a multifaceted activity that shifts depending on the situation. Other people become an audience, or 'co-participants' (1959: 27), made up of family, friends, work colleagues or strangers, who respond to performances and in turn can perform themselves. Thus, performance and impression management become part and parcel of how people negotiate their identities and social relations in daily life. Goffman is speaking of face-to-face encounters, so the idea of cultural or mediatized performance takes his original concept of the presentation of the self in everyday life into cultural and mediated situations.

What follows is an examination of the blurred boundaries between individual performers and collective performances by producers, participants and audiences in reality television. Gary Carter (2013) comments on the porosity of performance in reality shows where ordinary people 'come on in a performance mode. It's a symbiotic relationship between performer and producer, and then the position of performer as former audience'. This symbiotic relationship between producer, performer and audience is encapsulated in the casting of superfans as contestants in reality formats. The position of performer as former audience is the lifeblood of this entertainment genre.

PARTICIPATION

Television and radio has a history of ordinary people participating in entertainment shows. *Ordinary Television* by Francis Bonner (2003) charts the circular history of ordinary people as participants in television. In Australia, magazine-style light entertainment series of the 1970s and 1980s featured members of the public having a makeover or sharing a personal anecdote. In America, 'the confessional audience participation show emerged on radio in the years leading up to the end of World War II and remained popular on radio and TV throughout the 1940s and 1950s' (Watts 2009: 304). There was American postwar television like *Queen for a Day* (Mutual, NBC, ABC 1945–64, USA) or *Strike it Rich* (CBS 1947–58, USA) that combined competition with personal hardship. According to Watts, these 'misery quizzes' were not about ordinary participants' skills or knowledge but rather who had 'the saddest life story, expressing the greatest need, and generating the most audience applause and sympathy' (ibid.).

In the 1970s, the American *cinema verite* style of documentary, and the British fly-on-the-wall documentary tradition both gave ordinary people an opportunity to present a version of themselves in a story of their everyday lives. Documentaries such as *The Family* (BBC 1974, Paul Watson) filmed an ordinary working-class family, and, as Su Holmes (2010) points out, the notion of what was ordinary or working class about the family became a subject of discussion and criticism. She notes that viewers:

> saw the family become famous, responding to the press, TV and radio, and the wider barrage of media interest on screen. This created considerable debate and speculation about the effect of *The Family* on the Wilkinses' presentation of the self.
>
> (Holmes 2010: 262)

Grey Gardens (Albert and David Maysles, Ellen Hovde and Muffy Meyer 1976) filmed Big and Little Eadie Beale, a mother and daughter who were cousins of Jackie Onassis, living in a decaying East Hampton mansion in the state of New York. Gary Carter (2013) calls *Grey Gardens* an early example of reality TV because it gives the viewer a 'clear sense they are performing for the camera in a way that makes you feel really queasy'. This queasy feeling would become a feature of audience engagement with the genre.

Popular factual television in the 1990s borrowed from earlier forms of light entertainment and documentary, for example in using ordinary people to generate audience interest and evince emotions. In *Children's Hospital* (BBC1 1996–), one producer said 'we are making serious and considered documentary films' (Household 1998: 28, cited in Kilborn 2003: 97), and at the same time the series 'made extensive use of storytelling techniques familiar from the world of fictional medical soaps' (Kilborn 2003: 97). The representation of children and their families struggling to overcome difficult and emotionally challenging situations invited audiences to sympathize with these people, there but for the grace of God could be just like us. For example: 'I like programmes like *Children's Hospital*, I think it brings everyday life home to you' (35–50-year-old male); or 'I like *Children's Hospital* and I always end up in tears watching it but I always still watch it … I can't turn it off' (35–50-year-old female).

Popular factual television programmes usually featured cameras following ordinary people around in a normal environment, at work or at home, at the airport or as a tourist abroad. Thus, some notion of performance as everyday naturalistic behaviour was part of audience attitudes towards participants in reality television at this time. Take this comment made by a 12–15-year-old girl in 2000:

There's a programme, and they were following this girl around, she was from an estate and they went to her school and how she acts and, like, it was about her whole life. It was so interesting. I was so interested in watching it cos I was thinking it was so true. She didn't put on any act, it was completely her ... It was so good!

Cameras captured this person's 'whole life'. This viewer believed she was watching her everyday experience – 'it was completely her'. Such a response to a participant's natural behaviour on television echoes observational documentary claims that after a time people forget cameras are there. It also echoes 'reality television claims that people cannot convincingly pretend to be "other" for longer than about a week of surveillance' (Gary Carter 2014).

Truth claims were important to viewers in how they engaged with participants in popular factual entertainment at this juncture in time. Although the reality television of the late 1990s and early 2000s could be called entertainment, it didn't mean viewers thought everything was made up. For example in a survey of 8,216 adults in the UK aged 16–65+ in 2000, 50 per cent of respondents claimed that entertainment programmes about real people 'sometimes happen like this and are sometimes made up'; 12 per cent claimed these programmes 'really do happen like this' and only 2 per cent thought these programmes 'are all made up'. In terms of gender, 49 per cent of men and 51 per cent of women claimed these programmes 'sometimes happen like this and are sometimes made up'; for age the results were evenly spread across life stages (55 per cent aged 16–34; 51 per cent aged 35–54; 45 per cent aged 55+). For class, again the results were evenly distributed across upper- and higher-middle working class (53 per cent) and lower-middle to working class (48 per cent).

Audiences expected a docusoap to contain characters who acted as themselves and exaggerated themselves for the programme – a combination of 'sometimes happening like this' and 'sometimes made up'. Docusoaps were popular with audiences. In the same survey, 67 per cent of adult respondents aged 16–65+ liked 'observational programmes about watching people in everyday places'. In a survey of 937 respondents aged 4–15 (unweighted sample, 2000, UK) 67 per cent of children also claimed they liked these kinds of programmes. And yet, the majority of adult respondents also thought docusoaps were about real people performing themselves: 70 per cent of respondents claimed people acted up for the cameras in reality television programmes. In terms of gender, 71 per cent of men and 69 per cent of women respondents from the overall sample thought 'members of the public usually overact for the cameras'. For age and life stage, 74 per cent of 16–34 year olds, 71 per cent of 35–54 year olds and 65 per cent of over 55 year olds agreed with this statement. The distribution of respondents in relation to class was evenly spread across the upper and upper-middle classes (72 per cent) and middle to working classes (68 per cent).

Goffman (1959) claims impression management is a common feature of everyday life. Critics have counteracted this argument by pointing out that sustaining a favourable, perhaps deliberately false, impression of yourself is not a default position for social life (see Raffel 2013). What is more, keeping up an appearance can be stressful in routine behaviour, where one false slip reveals a side of the self we wish to remain private (Raffel 2013). The staged nature of the docusoap is not the everyday environment that Goffman had in mind. But for audiences, it can be an exaggerated environment that shows the stress of impression management. This male viewer imagined being filmed as a tourist in Ibiza's clubs: 'I'd be worse if I wasn't filmed! If I wasn't filmed, I'd be going mad but if I'm filmed I'd be like ... all quiet ... I don't like being filmed!' (35–50-year-old male).

Producer Jeremy Mills worked on the seminal docusoap *Airport* (BBC 1996–2008). He noted how 'you have to be able to predict the sort of response characters will have to a particular situation' (cited in Kilborn 2003: 97). Gary Carter (2014) comments:

> [B]efore you embark on a reality series, you know the participants well enough to be clear as to how they will respond in most situations. This is largely because you have a duty of care towards such participants as the maker, and largely because you are trying to construct circumstances with relatively controlled sets of outcomes.

Audiences could also reflect on characters' responses, judging reactions to social situations. In the 2000 survey, 36 per cent of adult respondents agreed with the statement 'I can always tell the difference between someone's story caught on camera, or being recreated for TV', whilst 45 per cent neither agreed nor disagreed with the statement. These female viewers (aged 18–34) discussed a scene from *Airport* that showed a couple at the check-in desk who had forgotten their son's passport:

Janice: I wouldn't expect that reaction in real life, to be honest, even though he was wrong I would have thought he would have argued a bit more.

Amy: He was very calm, wasn't he?

Tina: Although his voice was a bit shaky on the phone to his dad, I thought he was going to cry … I don't think it would be acted, I think it would be real …

Janice: Yeah, because there was emotion in his voice on the phone.

Bev: Perhaps he's just a calm person.

Tina: It's strange his wife didn't say anything, she didn't butt in and have a go or anything.

Amy: Can you imagine! I bet she's swearing at him after.

General: Yeah … [laughter]

Maggie: … Camera or no camera …

Tell-tale signs of a voice starting to crack, the eerily calm wife, indicate another reality off camera. So, alongside creative producers, viewers were also predicting the sort of response characters would have to a given situation and imagining both the television front (keep calm and carry on) and the reality backstage (a stand-up row).

Goffman's idea of presenting a better version of yourself in front of others becomes exaggerated in a television production. This is what some viewers mean when they talk about people acting up for the cameras, lifting up the good side of yourself, not wanting to look a fool. Misha Kavka (2008) argues that rather than acting up people in reality TV act out their emotions. Acting out is an overtly emotional performance that Kavka perceives as part of the reality genre. This is a useful distinction for competitive reality contestants in something like *America's Next Top Model* (CW 2003–). Acting out can mean playing up in front of the cameras, being overly aware of an emotional performance: 'I think people play up to the cameras, it's a natural reaction' (18–34-year-old male).

Subtle differences between acting up and playing up to the camera are significant to the performance modes of reality television. Acting up is more about wanting to create a good impression of yourself to others, perhaps keeping your emotions in check. Goffman's idea of the presentation of the self in everyday life is most applicable to this notion of acting up, an exaggerated form of a social role within the mediated 'world' space of reality television that we might see in programmes set around airports or hospitals. In this type of performance mode, participants and viewers are attuned to feeling rules of the kind Arlie Hochschild (2003) talks about in her work on a sociology of emotion. Small details matter in this kind of presentation of the self in reality television. Acting out, or playing up, is more about wanting to create an overt performance of yourself, perhaps letting your emotions run riot. Hochschild's subtle distinction between feeling rules and the expression of emotions is useful. In the 'television' space of reality programmes such as *America's Next Top Model* the participants draw on a bigger repertoire of emotional expressions, in particular negative emotions such as anger or jealousy. For Hochschild the differences in emotion are important. There is a fine line between being aware of feeling rules in social situations, trying to lower your voice, or repress anger, and expressing emotions in these same situations, shouting, or lashing out.

This female viewer (aged 16–34) explained:

> I think a lot of it's instinct as well ... most people you can tell just by looking at them, if they're playing up to the camera ... I mean, there's a lot of side glances to the camera if someone's having an argument. Say in *Airport*, if someone's having a massive argument with the checkout girl or something, you always see sneaky glances to the camera to say 'Are you watching?! Are you watching?!'

There is a distinction between the performance modes of acting up and acting out in reality television. People switch between feeling emotions, keeping them in check and expressing those emotions in public for television cameras.

The advent of *Big Brother* would alter attitudes towards participation and whether people acted up or played up to the cameras in a reality show. A conversation between two teenagers in 2000 highlighted shifting attitudes towards participating in a dating show at the time. *Streetmate* (Channel 4 1998–2001, UK) was presented by Davina McCall, the future face of *Big Brother* in Britain:

> Alison: It's not normal, do you know what I mean, like ... it's not normal to walk down the street and get stopped while you're shopping and someone come up to you and go 'right, come with me now, we'll find someone you think's fit and then you'll go out with them'. It doesn't happen! (12–15-year-old schoolgirl)
>
> Karen: And we're all sitting there thinking 'Oh, come to us!' (12–15-year-old schoolgirl)

It was not normal to be out shopping and suddenly find yourself participating in *Streetmate*. But that quick retort from her friend 'Oh, come to us!' hinted at changes to come.

Big Brother encouraged audiences to re-evaluate their attitudes towards participants in a reality show. It was hard to continue the argument that this was everyday life brought home to viewers on the sofa – *Big Brother* contestants were trying to win a cash prize and media attention. The first participants in *Big Brother* learned how to perform themselves, and at the same time compete in a gameshow, a strange mixture of naturalistic performances, for example sunbathing in the garden, and artificial behaviour, for example voting out other contestants. Later series illuminated a new performance mode – the participant as contestant. Gone was the notion of acting up to the camera – presenting a positive impression of yourself. Overt performance became a feature of the format: 'That's part of the show, innit, playing up to the camera and all that' (35–50-year-old male).

VOYEURS AND VIEWERS

Audiences of competitive reality shows were aware that producers, performers and viewers had entered into a different kind of relationship. Audiences drew on their genre knowledge of documentary or docusoap but these viewing modes did not match the hybrid style of competitive reality. For example, these female viewers (aged 18–34) talked about watching the first season of *Big Brother* in Britain:

Isobel: It was like a fly on the wall.
Jo: … You get embarrassed sometimes [laughs].
Angela: It would have been even more so if you'd just been inside someone's house without them knowing, though, wouldn't it really.
          [General laugh].

The feeling of embarrassment was key. This notion of peaking through the curtains, 'inside someone's house without them knowing', contained an implicit reference to surveillance and voyeurism. In early discussions about watching *Big Brother* the producer–audience relationship with participants-contestants took on sinister overtones.

Surveillance is a feature of reality television and critics have pointed out the political and ideological meanings to the genre as a whole. Following on from the analysis of reality programming by Bill Nichols (1994), debates about how people were represented in crime and surveillance series highlighted concern for the way producers' narrativized ordinary people and framed them in relation to certain political or social values. In surveillance series ordinary people do not simply perform themselves because law and order, or disciplinary, narratives situate people in a political and ideological frame. This idea of monitoring people was described by one female viewer (aged 18–34) as 'caught on camera, it really gives me the creeps'.

Big Brother typified surveillance culture, with its reference to the dystopian novel *Nineteen Eighty-Four* by George Orwell (1949). The format billed itself as a real-life soap, and 'created circumstances which would reveal the authenticity or otherwise of the participants' performances' (Carter 2014). Producers and audiences could monitor people in the house, modify behaviour of participants through tasks, and punish participants who did not follow the rules or were unpopular with the public. Surveillance and voyeurism touched on the blurring of public and private spaces; audiences were invited into an artificial environment in reality competition, where normally private behaviour, like taking a shower, was made public through surveillance cameras; audiences were then invited to pass judgement on this behaviour in the form of interactive voting and public debate. The narratives of *Big Brother*, such as surveillance and control, competition and commercialism, exhibition and exploitation, caused consternation amongst the public, with demonstrations against the premise of the show (see Mathijs 2002, Mathijs *et al.* 2004).

Mark Andrejevic's book *Reality TV: The Work of Being Watched* (2004) is based on a critical reading of surveillance culture. As a counteraction to celebratory rhetoric concerning reality television as democratic and participatory, Andrejevic unpacks the 'promise of power sharing' as a 'ruse of economic rationalization' (2004: 7). Far from being democratic, reality television has voyeuristic appeal in the form of exhibitionism and self-disclosure (2004: 174). Viewers of reality television are lulled into the work of being watched, a 'form of production wherein consumers are invited to sell access to their personal lives in a way not dissimilar to that in which they sell their labor power' (2004: 6). Viewers as voyeurs are co-opted by the entertainment industry into a surveillance economy.

Anita Biressi and Heather Nunn offer a more positive reading in *Reality TV: Realism and Revelation* (2005). They discuss the genre as narcissistic and a sign of a therapeutic culture:

> [T]he desire to be watched, to be witnessed by others uncovering one's intimate identity and even everyday rituals of cooking, eating, conversing, competing or sleeping reveals the craving for an observer to witness the minutiae of one's social performance.
>
> (2005: 101)

Biressi and Nunn refer to the fantasy of being watched by an 'other', not only as a sexual fantasy but also as a fantasy of the self to be validated through the media, to show we exist through the camera's gaze on our social life. 'Reality TV, then, arguably promotes and caters for the desire to be observed and to have one's existence validated through observation' (2005: 102). This connects an idea of a surveillance culture with a broad notion of subjectivity and identity as in some way driven by a desire to be seen and recognized in a mediated public space.

These debates about surveillance, voyeurism, narcissism and social observation were articulated by scholars, journalists and experts in newspapers, magazines, radio phone-ins and talkshows. One of the key issues with these debates is that 'few of the connotations of surveillance are positive' (McGrath 2004:1). Audiences echoed negative debates about the surveillance features of *Big Brother* – caught on camera 'gives me the creeps' – and observation of intimate settings – 'you get embarrassed'. Both frames of reference were, and still are, valid concerns about a hybrid genre that disregards public/private boundaries. However, ideas of surveillance and voyeurism dominated discourses to such an extent that there was little space for other frames of reference. McGrath points out that books like *Voyeur Nation* (Calvert 2000) were predicated on a critique of surveillance that grew out of 1990s research on crime prevention and privacy rights. Such a way of looking at surveillance is also ideological; it seems natural to be concerned about watching *Big Brother* because conventional structures of crime and privacy frame viewers as damaged by media voyeurism, or exploited by a surveillance economy (McGrath 2004: 203).

Jane Roscoe conducted production and audience research of the first season of *Big Brother* in Australia (Roscoe 2001). She noted (2013):

> Audiences felt like voyeurs. One of the first comments would be about voyeurism but people didn't understand the concept as it had been used in theoretical contexts, but in common parlance it actually was shorthand for 'I am just watching'. The idea of just watching was voyeurism as opposed to what was packed into that theoretical context. People didn't know how to express that.

There was an element of guilty viewing to watching the first season of *Big Brother* in Britain. *Big Brother* borrowed heavily from soap opera in its narrativization, characterization and editing styles. The show was criticized for being trashy and aimed at women more than men (it had a 60–40 split in favour of females, see Hill 2002). Moreover, it was thought to exemplify a voyeur nation. This meant that critics positioned *Big Brother* audiences as viewers who took pleasure from surveillance culture. Reality refusniks, the anti-fans of the genre, positioned *Big Brother* as lowest common denominator culture, watched by ignorant masses (see Hill 2007). It was no surprise to find viewers describing themselves as addicts, guilty about their TV habits.

Jane Roscoe (2013, 2001) presented an alternative frame of reference in her research on *Big Brother* producers and audiences in Australia:

> I always argued against voyeurism because in its strictest sense it does refer to sexual gratification and it didn't feel like that, even when you were watching *Big Brother* contestants half naked it felt like much more of a different relationship. They were aware of the cameras. It was a mutual consent we were engaged in performance and audience relationship. It was much more like going to the theatre than watching a dirty movie. Voyeurism didn't really ring true. This was a form of exhibitionism that needed an audience and it was OK to view that.
>
> (Roscoe 2013)

Similarly, McGrath (2004) argues for an alternative frame of reference to surveillance that draws on theatre, performance and art. He shows how the surveillance space of *Big Brother*, one where people perform multiple selves, can invite audiences to reflect on performance, where seeing nothing happen is a form of counter-surveillance – the more we see the less we know.

When conducting audience research at the time of the first season of *Big Brother* in Britain, nearly 10,000 children and adults were consulted through representative surveys, interviews and household observations. Much of the empirical evidence pointed to social drama rather than a surveillance culture. In a survey of 8,216 adults (aged 16–65+), 30 per cent were watching *Big Brother*: 28 per cent were male and 34 per cent were female viewers. In terms of age, 54 per cent were aged 16–34, 30 per cent were aged 35–54, and only 18 per cent were aged 55 and above. In terms of class, 35 per cent were upper and upper-middle class, and 30 per cent were middle to working class. Around half of these respondents in the survey claimed to like the social experience, such as watching the live events where ex-contestants were interviewed about their time in the house (59 per cent), watching the evening programme (55 per cent), choosing winners and losers (50 per cent) and talking about the show with family and friends (51 per cent) (see Hill 2002).

In terms of the target market for future competitive reality, 44 per cent of young respondents aged 4–15 claimed to like 'created for TV programmes' such as *Big Brother* (representative survey 2000, unweighted sample 937). This increased to 65 per cent of 10–15 year olds (unweighted sample 454). When asked what they liked about these kinds of programmes, younger respondents preferred social elements such as information about people (49 per cent), looking into other people's lives (43 per cent), arguments and disagreements (39 per cent) and reactions of the public (39 per cent), rather than intrusive cameras (25 per cent). For the teenage audience of 10–15 year olds, the percentages rose to around 50 per cent for the social elements in programmes like *Big Brother*, as opposed to intrusive cameras, at around 30 per cent. If we take the element of looking into other people's lives for all the young respondents in the survey, gender, age and class made little difference to their attitude towards liking the social drama of these programmes, for example 39 per cent of males and 48 per cent of females, and 46 per cent upper and upper-middle class compared to 43 per cent middle- and working-class respondents.

We might expect viewers to talk up the social side of watching *Big Brother*, wanting to give a positive impression as a counteraction against negative criticisms of voyeurism, or to appease their feelings as guilty viewers. But, when talking to viewers in their homes it became apparent they were processing a different kind of relationship between performer and audience. 'I'm just watching' did not carry sufficient clout in the heavily critical media debates about the format. Still, through the process of watching, audiences started to articulate a performative mode of engagement for competitive reality. The next section explores a competitive performance of the self, a 'did you see that!' moment where participants as contestants grab audience attention and generate media and social gossip.

THE MOMENT

In previous research on competitive reality various scholars have argued that performance and authenticity are essential to these formats. In John Corner's article titled 'Performing the Real' (2002: 263–64), he discusses the term selving as 'the central process whereby "true selves" are seen to emerge (and develop) from underneath and, indeed, through, the "performed selves" projected for us'. This alternation between the true self and performed self invites 'thick judgemental and speculative discourse around participants' motives, actions and likely future behaviour' (2002: 264). Corner's idea of selving connects with John McGrath's discussion of surveillance space as 'selves producing selves' (2004: 17). Lothar Mikos *et al.*, in their research of *Big Brother* in Germany, also suggested performance was key to understanding participants-contestants (Mikos *et al.*, 2000).

Roscoe described the process of selving as 'a glimmer of authenticity' within the performative frame of the format (2001). She explains how reality formats in the early 2000s invited audiences to reflect on 'selves producing selves':

> You heard people talk about the difference between how you are with some people and how you were at work. There was certainly moments where people would say they are just acting, and actually aren't we all like that all of the time. This was a moment when people could talk about multiple identities in meaningful ways whilst enjoying themselves. This wasn't a lecture, it wasn't a documentary on identity, but through just enjoying the banality of everyday life people started to talk about really interesting things. Audiences were drawing from performance, postmodern theories of identity, in ways we would not have identified in advance.
>
> (Roscoe 2013)

A glimmer of authenticity might be an example of what Goffman (1959) describes as the difference between the front-stage and back-stage self. For Goffman, the back-stage self can be the true self, but it can also be a consciously intimate glimpse into another identity we want to show friends, or family. Meyrowitz (1985) calls this a middle region between front and back stage, extending the notion of an authentic self as played out in mediated spaces. For Roscoe, reality television invited participants and audiences to play with multiple identities, reflecting on claims that all of us perform ourselves in the front stage, middle region and back stage of our mediated lives. She saw early audiences of *Big Brother* as exemplifying the ways people can detect a true or authentic inner self through 'thick judgemental and speculative discourse' on people's behaviour (Corner 2002).

There is a play off between authenticity and performance. A moment of authenticity in a performance is a crucial element of the 'reality' relations between producers, participants and audiences. An authentic moment can be a self-conscious performance of a 'true self'. But it can also be an exaggerated, or produced 'moment' of authenticity by a knowing participant cast by reality television producers. Before competitive reality, the genre had utilized common practices in documentary, or drama, to grab audience attention through unusual actions of real people, or memorable performances by actors. This young viewer described a 'did you see that!' moment in a docusoap about professional cleaners shown in 2000: 'I like *Life of Grime* cos it's the sort of thing you can go in next day and talk to your friends, "Uurgh, did you see the scanky house with all that dog poo?!"' (15-year-old school boy). Another young viewer went on to describe how *Big Brother* producers approached the challenge of capturing audience attention: 'If it's like boring, you're not going to watch so they've got to keep you interested with things you haven't seen before, that shock or amaze you, not just, like, some man buying some sweets in a shop!' (12-year-old schoolboy).

As we can see from these young viewers, competitive reality added an extra dimension to the 'did you see that!' moment in traditional television. It took the idea of selving and exaggerated it in order to encourage the public to watch, interact and vote. We can call this 'the moment' – the moment when someone performing themselves shows us a glimpse of an alternative reality hidden behind the façade. For the first season of *Big Brother* in Britain the moment was associated with Nasty Nick's eviction from the house. For some time viewers had been aware that Nick had been lying about his past and manipulating contestants. He was finally confronted, broke down in tears and was evicted for cheating. These female viewers (aged 18–34) commented:

> Amy: I mean it's laughable now but at the time it was 'Oh, my god!'
> General: Yeah.
> Amy: I phoned my friend up and I was very upset! [laughs] I went I've seen someone nearly have a nervous breakdown!
> Janice: And everybody was talking about it as well.

This episode in the first season of *Big Brother* exemplified the elements of 'the moment' that would become commonplace in competitive reality formats. There was the casting of a character audiences loved to hate. Tabloid papers called him Nasty Nick because of his blatant deception. There were the multiple identities contained within the performances of participants and the editing by producers to draw out these selves. Nick was performing a friendly version of himself in front of housemates, but producers revealed a devious back-stage self to audiences. There were interactive viewers and users. The public tuned in to watch this episode and the live eviction show, voting for or against people they loved or hated. They took a closer look at the house via webcams, all the time speculating about his character, weighing up his multiple identities and gossiping about him as a person and a contestant. And then there was the media attention given to this moment, reported in the news, featured in magazines and hotly debated on talkshows, repackaged and remediated for maximum impact.

The moment in early seasons of *Big Brother* was genuinely something new to audiences. 'There was a sense these programmes gained access to something completely different. That is the thing we talk about and remember' (Roscoe 2013). One female viewer (aged 18–34) commented on the Nasty Nick moment as: 'the thing is, it's real life ... you're not watching some soap character, sort of have some crisis over absolutely nothing. You're watching someone's life, aren't you?' The authenticity of the moment was significant; this was someone's real life set within the parameters of a reality show. And the intimacy of the moment was significant, a glimpse into a private space not often revealed to the public. These young female viewers (aged 12–15) explained:

> Sam: Yeah. I like felt sorry for him because of his crying but it was sort of like it made something better, it was a good thing cos ... yeah, it made everyone watch it.
> Jenny: Yeah, but people may have feelings, it's not like it's a soap opera, it's real life.

This moment of authenticity was understood as an emotional performance, a glimpse of intimate relations played out in a mediated public space.

The relationship between creative producers, participants and audiences consolidated around these reality TV moments. When Gary Carter (2013) describes this relationship as symbiotic, he is referring to the co-production of these performances. Producers consciously cast characters and created situations where a 'did you see that!' moment might occur; participants consciously played up their personalities to generate memorable moments, an example of what McGrath calls 'selves producing selves' (2004: 17); and audiences engaged in a social performance where 'everyone was talking about it'. The moment quickly became overproduced. For example, these 12–15-year-old schoolgirls speculated on whether Nasty Nick was a plant:

> Jo: I think that *Big Brother* planted him there ... cos without that, without him, can you imagine ... *Big Brother* would have been really boring.
> Amy: Yeah, they've got to get someone there to make it interesting.
> Chris: Unless they paid him, unless he was a genuine person and they paid him to, like, start making trouble. Because they weren't even angry at him or anything, *Big*

Brother were like 'So, how do you feel?' You wouldn't say that to someone, you'd say 'What are you doing?! You're a nutter! What are you mucking up your chances for?!'

What was genuine about these moments in competitive reality quickly degenerated into something forced that invited suspicion rather than speculation from viewers.

THE MOMENT'S MOMENT

A moment's moment is big theatre. It is the point at which the small moments we talk about in a reality show become manufactured as big memorable moments. In *American Idol* (Season 11, 2012) judge Randy Jackson described the emotional breakdown of contestant Joshua Ledet as a 'moment's moment'. In the semi-finals Jackson commented on Phillip Phillip's performance: 'Finally, in the end, in this moment, when you need moments … you had a giant moment' (Herman 2012). For Jackson, a contestant's emotional investment in a live performance (the moment) is combined with the framing of this performance as a memorable moment within the television show and cross-media. The 'moment's moment' is a strategic move by producers to deliver a big emotional performance. This 'moment's moment' then becomes an aggregation of moments that feature in a live show, 'best of' segments from the series, YouTube videos and social media chatter. Gary Carter (2013) explains this feature of talent formats as 'the moments full of moments – take all the best moments and we stitch them together into another great moment'. The moment's moment is 'faux and stagey and utterly illegitimate' (Carter 2013).

There are several elements that come together in the strategic production of a moment's moment, and an aggregation of these moments full of moments in competitive reality. First there is the use of participants as contestants – ordinary people we have not seen before suddenly having their chance in the spotlight. Douglas Wood (2013), Head of Audience Research at Shine Group, commented on 'the Gareth Gates moment' in the first season of *Pop Idol* in the UK (ITV1 2001). Gates auditioned for *Idol*, gathered a fanbase, and went on to become runner-up in the live series finale:

> You started to see people trying to replicate those moments. The emotional back story, the nervous contestant, the mother waiting in the wings, the powerful audition following a false start. When you do it too many times the impact of this moment becomes lost.

This is a back-stage to front-stage performance of the self, where the audience is positioned as talent scout.

Another element is the reactions of judges to auditions and live performances in talent formats. Julie Donovan (2013), a formats consultant, noted how 'you see the artificial arguments in the judging panels in the shows. When you feel like you are being over manipulated you fall out of love with the shows'. The judges react to the supposedly authentic performance of a participant, that inner self we see a glimpse of, and manipulate the moment to the point of saturation. A third element is the big emotions that accompany these performances by participants and judges. Jane Roscoe, Head of International Sales, SBS, Australia, (2013) explains:

> It is like the reveal in the makeover show. You have to have this moment, and usually in a competition it is when someone breaks down and cries, and not just a few tears, you have got to have traumatic moments. That is part of how it has evolved. These moments of extreme emotions are absolutely necessary in competition shows.

Moments of extreme emotions are experienced by participants and then fed back, like emotional reverb, through the reactions of judges, a live crowd and the viewing public.

In this way, the moment's moment is a combination of performance, reaction and extreme emotion. It is also a trope for talent formats. Carter comments:

> You might call this the Susan Boyle effect, a trope that enters the system ... What made Susan Boyle different was YouTube. Everyone wants a moment's moment for YouTube. And YouTube has genre

specifications because it has conventions. If what you are looking for, consciously or unconsciously as a performer, is media exposure you are going to be complicit with that trope because you know how to package yourself.

The Gareth Gates moment, 'someone is coming in who you think is rubbish but you know they will be amazing', evolves into the Susan Boyle effect where her audition in *Britain's Got Talent* becomes a mega moment, re-mediated as a trope for YouTube.

Roscoe (2013) describes the trope in talent formats as the big shiny floor moment:

> You have a factory of formats and each one has to be bigger and better. These formats are massive productions and every little detail is controlled, the way they communicate, there is nothing left to chance. On the one hand it might give viewers a satisfying experience, it is a really well made shiny floor show. On the other hand why it feels less interesting to other viewers is that it is too manufactured, too perfect. There is very little space for surprise. If we talk in TV about the job to surprise and delight viewers, for formats you do that with big name judges, fireworks, a big band, but you don't do it through those little moments that you don't expect, like wow she is different than I expect. You get the big shiny floor moment that is manufactured, and it has to be that way because everywhere around the world they want the same experience.

The big shiny floor moment becomes branded within a format and fed into a spiral of cross-media content.

Audiences are aware of a transition from something that seems like an emotionally authentic moment to an overproduced mega moment. There is 'loud and shrieky' television of the kind where 'there is no structure except what the performers themselves are delivering' (Gary Carter 2013). *The Only Way is Essex* or *Keeping up with the Kardashians* (E! 2007–, USA) are good examples of this kind of scripted reality programming. This term usually 'means that the storyline is created and the performers are "improvising" in that frame, "playing" themselves' (Gary Carter 2014).

In the following discussion, viewers reflected on the manufactured moment:

Jack: I think they're looking for drama, to get the viewers to be like 'oh my god, I can't believe I just saw that'. (24-year-old sound technician)

Debora: Like if it's real, you can tell with certain programmes how they edit it, like, it's very TV but it's more like a soap. You get that kind of entertainment ... (19-year-old sales assistant)

Jessie: Just think about it, there are those types of people who act their way through most of their lives ... (21-year-old male artist)

Jon: I mean they might, kind of, act out for the camera, but then you know they end up off camera so at some point they are just going to be themselves. (24-year-old unemployed person)

Debora: ... It's not so much that they are just acting, it's like the situations are set up so they *will* react in a certain way ...

Fiona: They want to portray a certain character a certain way, to push them and push them. (19-year-old student)

Debora: Yeah, so then they're trapped.

Here then, ordinary people performing themselves become trapped in the artificial environment of the show. When June Deery (2012) talks about branding in reality TV, this is what audiences have in mind in the manufacturing of artificial personalities. Performers are acting out, producing meta versions of themselves they assume producers and audiences want to see.

Around the time of the first seasons of *Big Brother* and *Pop Idol* in Britain, a common phrase used in discussion of participants-contestants was 'good luck to them'. Time and again audiences would reflect on what it must be like to participate in competitive reality, and although there was concern about a fifteen minutes of fame syndrome, people would end discussions with a note of cautious optimism – good luck to them. It says something about the goodwill of audiences towards participants in early seasons of talent formats. By the mid-2000s it was hard to find positive comments by audiences on reality TV participants. In a relatively short space of time viewers turned on these people (see Hill 2007). Douglas Wood explained, 'it is that sense of desperation. Many of the contestants were no longer ordinary people. They had lost their innocence and became fame hungry, carbon-copy talent show characters, just brazen about why they were there' (2013). This viewer summed it up: 'Well, it's all sensationalizing somebody's life even though they're a bit of a twat' (25-year-old female writer).

In a short space of time audience engagement with the performance of the self in reality TV transformed from the little moments into big theatrical moments. This is the 'flip side of flickers of authenticity' (Roscoe 2013). These moments are full on: 'you are engaged in a completely different way, they are really big, they take up the full screen, take up the space' (Roscoe 2013). There is little room for audiences to find their own way of engaging with people, or using thick description to think through social relations. 'No one is interested in "well I tried my best and that is that". You want the big tears. Small tears are not enough in telly, you want the big tears' (Roscoe 2013). The presenter of *Strictly Come Dancing: It Takes Two* (2013) described the big moments in this format as 'tears, tantrums and tens'.

The manufacturing of the moment's moment is part of the reason why ratings for talent formats are in decline, and audiences and critics bemoan their predictability. For example, the second season finale of *The Voice* (BBC1 2013) attracted around seven million viewers on a Saturday night in Britain. On average the series had around five million viewers, down from eight million for the previous year. The official BBC blog described the finale as 'the greatest finals in the history of finals' (BBC 2013). *Guardian* television critic Stuart Heritage (2013b) disagreed. He led his live blog with 'prop yourself up everyone. This is going to be tedious'. In many ways the moment full of moments in reality formats has become so overblown there is no space left for audiences to make these shows their own.

CONCLUSION

Beverly Skeggs and Helen Wood (2012) have shown how significant reactions are to understanding reality TV: the reactions of people as they perform in the media, the reactions of critics and the public to these performances. In their study of women watching lifestyle makeover series such as *Wife Swap* in the mid-2000s, the reactions of viewers highlighted how affect is central to the genre. Indeed, they argue an unintentional consequence of reality television's focus on emotional performance is that the genre makes an intervention into the production of subjectivity. For example, programmes such as *Wife Swap* contain performances of personhood. Reality television does not set out to intervene in our reactions to personhood, but through inviting audiences to assess performances they are 'put in the position of the judge' and at the same time judged on their reactions to participants (2012: 222). They note 'rarely, in other areas of our lives, do we watch the performative broken down and staged over time and space' (ibid.). Reality television's 'invitation to the viewer to unpack person performance' offers up 'moments for critical attention' and thus 'enables audiences to see how utterly incoherent, contradictory and unstable the production of subjectivity and normativity is' (ibid.).

Reality television's focus on the performative broken down and staged over time is richly suggestive. There are people performing themselves and social roles, such as parent, pop star or entrepreneur. Such a moment when we can watch the performance of selves and social roles relies on producers and participants allowing space for what we can call 'the moment', those personal details that we pick up on and say 'did you see that!' One female viewer (a 21-year-old student) in the mid-2000s explained, 'You get these insights to their reaction I think, and that's what you have to feed off, that's what you get given really, because you know that's all you're given.' Skeggs and Wood's emphasis on reaction as an affective economy in the genre is precisely what this viewer notices in their moment of critical attention to performance. John Corner's discussion of selving in *Big Brother* becomes especially relevant as this viewer knows their primary mode of engagement with the genre is through thick judgemental description of performance and personhood. Skeggs and Wood reject the viewer as voyeur interpretation of the genre. They criticize ideologies of surveillance, or governance, as the primary means of analysing reality television because their empirical evidence suggests something else. Audiences are constantly breaking down notions of watching, reacting and performing; positioning themselves, often in contradictory ways, as both a judge of participants in reality TV and the object of judgement by others watching these shows.

With the development of competitive reality as mega formats, producers and participants took the significance of reaction and turned it into a trope. Think of 'the Susan Boyle effect' where reactions from the judges and the live crowd to Boyle's audition in *Britain's Got Talent* were manufactured into a moment full of moments that were YouTube friendly. If you search YouTube for this first audition it comes with the tag 'big surprise'. In this way, reacting to performance in reality TV has become a trope within the system. If the genre, at one point in its development, unintentionally triggered an intervention into ideologies of subjectivity, identity and performance in everyday life, then in its current form there is an intentional manufacturing of performance and our reactions to personhood. John McGrath in 2004 argued that the practice of 'selves producing selves' in theatre or art, using CCTV footage or video diaries, could be a new form of consciousness for living in a surveillance space. The moment's moment is what happens when a factory of formats manufactures this practice of selving. If all we get given in talent formats are big tears, big tantrums, big surprise, then what do audiences have left to feed off? Without the little moments you don't expect in people's performance of themselves, reality formats minimize the multiple ways we engage with this kind of media.

4

REALITY TV EXPERIENCES

The celebrity cult, it's mental.

(35-year-old male printer)

Reality TV drives an experience economy. As an entertainment genre, it ensures that a live reality event, programme or format not only has economic value but emotional value as an interactive experience embedded in people's lives (Pine and Gilmore 2011). Audiences for reality TV are able to experience media in such a way that they participate in the process itself as consumers, performers, participants and producers. In many ways, audience experiences of reality TV, and other media in general, parallel those cultural experiences offered to fans for live sporting events. Audiences are positioned as supporters rather than consumers, as part of and not extra to an event (Boyle and Haynes 2009).

Philip Napoli claims in *Audience Evolution* (2010) that media managers must understand audience practices if they are to survive the rapid changes occurring in the marketplace. Media professionals are entering into a complex relationship with their consumers-audiences-producers. Reality formats such as *The Voice* or *Dancing on Ice* highlight how audiences can be both consumers and participants in an immersive media environment, able to support and vote for contestants during live broadcasts, perform during auditions and live events, produce and create mobile and online media content, and consume merchandizing, music and other media, such as spin-off shows, magazines and newspapers. The liveness of competitive reality formats is a significant feature of a new reality television economy. Little used in early forms of reality television in the 1990s, which relied on immediacy as a proxy for liveness, the live event status of this specific kind of reality television is worthy of close analysis (see Corner 2011). Audience's evolving experience of live reality television is richly suggestive for thinking about how media producers, professional reality TV contestants, celebrities and audiences co-create live cross-media content.

EXPERIENCE ECONOMY

The Experience Economy (Pine and Gilmore 2011) charts business trends that go beyond goods and services. The subtitle of the first edition spells out the message: 'work is theatre and every business a stage' (1999). 'The greatest opportunity for value creation resides in staging experiences' (2011: ix–xviii). Examples include tourism and boutique hotel experiences. Pine and Gilmore argue that the experience economy comes at a key moment when knowledge, attention and creativity are of high social and economic value. They give the example of birthday parties; whereas only a few decades ago parents would bake a cake, decorate a home and organize games for their children's birthday parties, now time-poor parents are willing to pay for a birthday party experience from event companies, fast food outlets or petting zoos. 'Staging compelling experiences begins with embracing an experience-directed mindset' (2011: 27). This mindset includes 'sensorialising the goods' on offer by heightening the sensory experience for customer interaction, and increasing opportunities for membership and participation (ibid.). Companies can also 'stage goods events', often through live and interactive experiences (ibid.). Although Pine and Gilmore emphasize the staging of experiences for companies, they acknowledge the role of 'co-creation in the formation of experiences' using terms such as participation and prosumer to highlight the multiplicity of dimensions to engaging, multisensory and memorable experiences (2011: xx).

The Experience Economy was first published at a time when reality TV took off as formatted entertainment. It is no coincidence that the reality genre shifted from infotainment in the early 1990s to an emphasis on drama and performance, with multiple points of narrative, characterization, engagement and interaction (see Glynn 2000; Hill 2005, 2007). Around the turn of the millennium, Napoli (2010) describes a media industry in crisis, with audience fragmentation across different kinds of content, media ownership and regulation in flux, and the rise of the internet as a major rival to audience attention. Reality television producers finely tuned an already existing play between fact and fiction, performance and engagement, in reality soaps like MTV's *The Real World* and formatted this mix into live mediated experiences.

There were formats before the success of *Big Brother*, *Idols*, or *Strictly Come Dancing*. The following viewers (aged 18–44) commented on lifestyle TV like *Changing Rooms* (BBC, UK) in the late 1990s:

Mark: I find that too orchestrated now, it's the same format every time ... you know what's coming and you know how it's going to end and I don't enjoy it for those reasons, really.

Andrew: It's had its day really, hasn't it. It was all right at first, weren't it?

Mark: Yeah, you watch the first two minutes and you watch the last two minutes and you've seen the programme.

But, competitive reality changed the market for entertainment formats.

There are several reasons why formats took off at the turn of the millennium. Briefly, independent producers were able to sell shows to broadcasters whilst retaining rights to the idea itself – the format. From this new kind of intellectual property rights, format-driven companies were able to grow into powerful international businesses that acquired, created, produced, marketed and distributed formats around the world. Rather than create an idea for a new show from scratch, networks, broadcasters and cable channels could reduce their economic risks through buying a show with a proven track record. What the industry call 'shiny floor shows' like *Strictly Come Dancing* have a certain look and feel, a production bible, that comes from the format originator, but can be made to measure for other regions, countries and cultures (Hill and Steemers 2011). In terms of the experience economy, reality formats transformed 'people TV' into live events where audience interaction was embedded in the format.

Some companies have to think creatively about how to sensorialize their goods and services. Pine and Gilmore talk in awe about Duct Tape experiences, where something so mundane as grey sticky tape used to fix a variety of household parts is given a makeover as a 'reliable friend' within an experience economy. Reality formats put emotion and performance centre stage. Here the drama of a live entertainment show for a large crowd is utilized for maximum affect. There are emotional, physical and vocal performances, judging performance skills, and the performance of people participating in the show as themselves, as contestants and as live crowds and audiences. Interactive elements include phone and internet voting, chatting, creating and sharing content through social media, or gaming. The sensorializing of the format and the interactive elements like public voting are steps towards the central staging of live media experiences, key to the success of many reality shows. For example *Dancing on Ice* (ITV1, UK) asks viewers to watch a live show, vote for their favourite celebrity ice skaters to stay in the competition, score the performances using a free mobile application, join in the live official Facebook and Twitter sites, download free music and video files featured during the season, attend the live show and buy tickets for the national tour.

This viewer defined these kinds of reality formats as follows:

> I've got this tight interactive section – *The X Factor, Big Brother* ... they rely basically, totally, on viewer participation as much as watching. You've got to call. These shows couldn't work if they didn't have people calling and stuff like that. That's how they make their money.
>
> (21-year-old male writer)

Tight interactivity is a good way of describing reality formats. For example, from the moment of auditions *The X Factor* begins with a high degree of audience and performer interaction. Early on, auditions were filmed behind closed doors but later seasons opened up the auditions process to a live audience in theatrical venues to heighten interaction. The feeling of liveness is produced even in these pre-recorded segments through the participation of the contestants and their family and friends as supporters, coupled with the judging panel positioned front of stage, and back-stage presenters and producers. Once the live shows begin the interactive elements are part of an event that carries audiences through to the season finale. Tight interactivity is a key driver for audience engagement through a long season that can include as many as twenty to thirty shows. This viewer explained:

> *The X Factor, The Apprentice*, which you have to kind of watch it every week to appreciate it … You have to know the characters to appreciate it more. It's more of an investment. And you kind of decide 'yeah, I'm going sign up for that'.
>
> (38-year-old female office assistant)

Napoli (2010) charts media industry trends in an attention economy or experience economy. He analyses the transformation of audience information systems, such as ratings, audience appreciation and measures of engagement. Industry audience research analyses engagement as attention, memory, emotions and social relations (2010: 100). In particular, 'audiences' emotional responses to content have also been posited as a central element of the broader concept of engagement' (ibid.: 104). Performance metrics are applied to television content, for example emotional engagement in drama, recall of adverts, or mood detection for Twitter feeds. Napoli describes the current state of institutional audience research as chaotic attempts to respond to changing dynamics of media consumption, such as increased fragmentation, interactivity and autonomy. He predicts a future of 'greater narrative complexity and ambiguity in our cultural products' where 'the narrative experience associated with any media product extends beyond the primary medium for which it was produced' (ibid.: 155).

Reality talent formats are examples of the way media managers and producers can extend narrative experiences beyond the show

Andy: In the end, it's like watching *Coronation Street* or *EastEnders*, innit.

Michael: Yeah but *Coronation Street* and *EastEnders* are fictional. It's there to try and bring you entertainment. That is supposed to be a fly-on-the-wall, cameras following their every move.

Andy: It was all about hype and marketing and getting the advertising and I'm sure the programme producers are rubbing their hands with glee!

Chris: That's what most telly is anyway, innit, at the end of the day. Innit? They're not gong to make a programme that no one wants to watch, are they?

Colin: It's never been done before, that sort of voyeurism. And it was so compulsive. It'll be one of the major programmes that'll be remembered this year.

Paul: You can hire the house out now for your Christmas party.

If we compare reality TV with sports, there are similar trends in the commercialization of entertainment for mass audiences. For example, the 'configuration of football fandom arguably changed dramatically during the 1990s with the widening points of consumption of all things football – whether in all-seater stadiums, subscription sports channels, replica kits or the web' (Boyle and Haynes 2009: 194). Faced with a major crisis, the sports industry turned to its fans and supporters and created 'a sense of belonging in an era of change' (ibid.: 201). Sports fandom is a 'highly mediated sporting experience' (ibid.: 198). But, even if experiences such as those in the sports industry are commercialized and commodified they can still 'involve other forms of experience and exchange – to do with shared experience, with popular memory, with a sense of place and space' (Whannel 2007: 150, cited in Boyle and Haynes 2009: 198). The next section explores how reality TV sells live media experiences that are not always structured and controllable by producers or marketers.

EMOTIONAL ENGAGEMENT

In sports, critics talk about passion play. Reality TV is also a genre that plays with passions. Dramatic construction of strong storylines that pack an emotional punch works alongside moments of real human experience. This viewer compared sports and reality TV:

> Well, it's that thing about the British public, we like to watch on TV people's downfalls ... you know, hand on heart, I'm one of those people ... you can't deny it, we like to see people on TV, we like to see their downfalls. You know, like Posh and Becks. Now everyone gives them grief. I mean, don't get me wrong, when David Beckham first came on the scene people said 'oh, just give him stick on the terraces!' But I think the geezer's great. Hand on heart, my heart bled for him when he came back from the World Cup, all because he did one mistake. As they say, football is more important than life or death. He did one mistake and the whole country was after him. His family was getting threatened. Why? ... We all make mistakes!
>
> (37-year-old male train driver)

Both *Big Brother* and David Beckham have been credited with revolutionizing economics, culture and sport. Cashmore (2004) describes the celebrity status of Beckham as situated in a key historical moment in the commodification of football and pay-per-view services for Premier League and satellite and cable television. 'The commodified Beckham' (2004: 192) is one part of the structuring of this passion play. There is also his dramatic narrative of 'trial and tribulation, victory and defeat, humiliation and redemption' (Boyle and Haynes 2009: 90). This narrative is in turn connected to passionate fans and supporters drawn to participation in sport. Similarly, reality formats like *Big Brother* were successful at a particular moment in the commercialization of television, mobiles and the internet. Reality TV participants in these kinds of formats have dramatic narratives and incite strong emotional responses. A passion play of love and hate is performed and consumed by reality TV viewers in a visible and vocal mediated space.

Emotions are central to understanding 'in your face' 'contrived factual entertainment' (Kilborn 2003: 74). The construction of emotions in reality TV involves the cultural practices of producers, participants and audiences working together. We can say this is a co-production of emotional performances. There is the production of performances through characterization, narrative and editing. For example, one producer of a docusoap described the casting of 'big characters with small stories to tell' (Kilborn 2003: 97). Performance also means the acting ability of real people who perform themselves for the purposes of entertainment. A series producer of a formatted reality show in the late 1990s noted how participants adapted to the contrived situation of the programme. *Living With the Enemy* (BBC2, UK) challenged people with wildly different values to spend a week together – animal rights activist versus hunter. The producer observed people improvising their roles as antagonists. Participants rehearsed during the week, sounding each other out, identifying the emotional triggers that would create disagreement: 'they don't just turn up and start arguing' (Kilborn 2003: 165). And performance refers to a more general sense of the roles we play as professionals, friends, parents, in our everyday lives (see previous chapter). Kilborn suggests the success of reality TV is connected to 'the pleasure that audiences take in measuring the subject's ability to generate an appropriate performance as a reflection of that real-life role-playing in which all of us are required to indulge on a daily basis' (2003: 14).

Research on performances in theatre or documentary that are based on real people emphasize the centrality of emotions to ways audiences engage in the authenticity of a drama (see Lipkin 2002; Cantrell and Luckhurst 2010). Whereas actors performing real people invite audiences to think about how fact might become fiction, reality TV also asks audiences to reflect on how fiction might become fact. In a survey of 4,516 respondents in 2003, around 70 per cent expected people to perform in reality shows. When asked if it was important people did not act up for the cameras, only one-third of respondents agreed with this statement. Key is the genre expectation that reality TV is dramatized. As few as 11 per cent of respondents in this sample claimed reality formats were true to life. As this woman explained, 'programmes such as *Big Brother* are not factual because the contestants are in a false environment and are acting up for the camera' (aged 25–34).

Reality performances are distinct from actors performing in docudrama. But they are not entirely fictional. One viewer said: 'I think the way in which people speak is more realistic than scripted. The kind of active-style dialogue. I think that's one thing that makes it feel much more realistic' (22-year-old female bar staff). Active-style dialogue is a good description of reality performances. Another viewer imagined what it must be like to be a participant:

> I mean, when the camera's on you all the time it's boring because it hasn't got a plot. We haven't rehearsed something. But when you've been, when you rehearse and you say 'well, we have to do this and we have to do that, the cameras are going to point at us', then ... you know, you give something to the people.
>
> (29-year-old male electrician)

Kilborn (2003: 102) calls this the 'Actuality Plus' frame of reference for audiences: 'an acknowledgement of the fact that producers will have dramatically and creatively enhanced the reality being projected'.

Alongside 'active-style dialogue', voice and dance are significant performative modes in reality talent formats. Paget and Roscoe (2006) in their research on another hybrid form, the docusmusical, argue for greater attention to sound in documentary studies. They draw on Altman's (1992) idea of 'point of audition' to work alongside 'point of view' in their analysis of the documusical. 'Music, as in drama, has a linking/commentating function, driving narrative and providing emotional texture. As John Corner has observed, music in documentary "greatly intensifies our engagement with ... images"' (2006). For Paget and Roscoe music extends the range of emotional colour within documentary, in particular voice performance can feel more authentic to audiences, a shortcut to an 'emotional hub' (ibid.). Shows like *The X Factor* draw on vocal performance to intensify that sense of 'emotional truth' producers are looking for in reality television performances. This is not so much a true emotion, but the production of an emotional indicator of broader human and social truths. These viewers (aged 20–30) commented:

> Emma: Some of them are real feelings as well. I mean, these, what's it called ... for example *The X-Factor*, all of those, that's real feelings. People are in there for a reason. It's that they want to become famous.

Chris: That's the driving thing, everybody wants to be famous.

Emma: So, they are really emotional, passionate.

Physical performances are another shortcut to an emotional hub. In sports attention has been paid to a 'point of contact' or a kinetic energy to physical performances. For example, one sports critic commented, 'boxing has a smell coming off it, and a feel ... the taste and sometimes the stink of sweat, snot and blood as bodies clash and clinch' (Boyle and Haynes 2009: 142). To really experience boxing you have to be there ringside. For televized boxing, drama is enhanced in 'the ritual of the pre-fight weigh in, the menacing eye-to-eye stares', or theatrical entrances to the boxing ring (ibid.). Similarly, physical performance is enhanced in televized live reality shows. In *Got to Dance* (Shine Group, Sky One 2012, UK) a teenage boy talked about his love of contemporary dance and how this private passion was a cause of bullying in school. When he performed his dance routine everyone was moved to tears, the studio audience, the presenter and judges, and viewers were invited to extend their own range of emotional engagement through responding to his dance. As with so many physical or vocal performances in reality talent shows, it is not so much this performer's technical skill or level of professionalism that is at stake, but their ability to express something that feels authentic, to move us in some way.

In the 2012 season of *American Idol* the judges repeatedly emphasized that vocal skill was not enough to win; contestants needed to make an emotional connection through their vocal performances. In one live show (episode 19) several contestants broke down whilst performing. As judge Jennifer Lopez said, 'I feel you, baby'. So powerful were their vocal performances that the panel of judges stood up countless times in appreciation. For a professional singer there is a balance between expressing emotion and losing control of their voice. Time and again viewers will vote for contestants who have struggled with a vocal performance, or tripped up in a ballroom dance routine, as long as they can express through physical and vocal performances their 'real feelings', what's driving them to win, how 'really emotional, passionate' they are.

Reality TV, and live talent formats in particular, is specifically designed to extend an audience's range of emotional modes of engagement. Paget and Roscoe (2006) write that the documusical 'enhances both the reach and grasp of documentary. Through this innovation in form, documentary has moved towards a fresh acknowledgement of the complexities in a mediatized society inherent in truth-in-representation'. Reality TV extends the reach and grasp of truth in representation. It offers an emotional truth that is part fact part drama. In the following discussion by viewers (aged 20–30) we can see how people respond to the complexities of this hybrid cultural form:

Evelyn: It is a recreated scenery, and something unfolds in real time, but it's not a real situation.

Samual: Yeah, the ones that are on now are formula programmes. But I think when it started reality TV wasn't like that necessarily. It was more like just a type of documentary making. It was very much based on observation.

Kevin: Voyeurism.

Samual: And now it's much more structured and it's more, like, deliberately made entertaining.

Kevin: Humiliating the sort of people in it.

Samual: Yeah.

Kevin: In the unreal situation.

Samual: Which makes it less real. Because it's like …

Kevin: … formula.

Samual: Yeah, unreal. People trying to act normally on purpose, but they're kind of acting.

Kim: They know they're being watched.

Stephen: They're acting. It's not actually real.

Kevin: What is real? (laughter)

Kim: Well, it's real people and it's a real situation. But it's an unnatural situation. I mean, it's happening, it's real, it's there. They are there, everything's live. Whatever they do, whether they …

Ollie: It's live, but …

Evelyn: No I think it's not real. It's constructed in a way, so it looks ...

Kim: It's real. I mean, they are there.

Evelyn: Yeah, but I mean ...

Kevin: They're heavily directed and planned, and in a way they're trying to create a drama but without a script. You know, and they just kind of create, sort of sign posts for the people. It's like an alternative to drama without the expense and time for writing a script, I think.

Liz: It's a bit like a soap opera, actually.

Ollie: I think it's better because you actually see people suffering. You know, it makes it better. It's like an ancient formula in a different format. It's just human nature. That's what it is.

This rich example highlights the practices of emotional engagement for reality TV. There is reflection on truth-in-representation. There is an emphasis on emotion and performance. There is a debate about editing, scripting, direction – the structuring of reality. There is close attention to acting styles, live television and its sense of presence, and the tensions inherent in performing reality drama. The emphasis on drama here underscores the staging of reality within this kind of television. And there is reflection on human experience in a mediated society.

CELEBRITY EXPERIENCE

Much discussion has arisen surrounding the tricky issue of ordinary people becoming celebrities within reality TV, such as winners of reality talent shows, or professional reality performers like the Kardashians, and celebrities competing and performing in reality formats, such as the winners of *Strictly Come Dancing*. Suffice to say the promise of a celebrity experience is a complex component of the reality genre. If the genre widens points of engagement for consumers, users and audiences through its focus on performance and interaction, the use of celebrities and ordinary people can work both for and against an emotional hub. This is because audiences, fans and anti-fans do not see the contestants in competitive reality as ordinary people performing themselves, but rather these are professional reality contestants, many of whom have grown up with talent shows and target these formats as vehicles for a mediatized performance of the self. Similarly, audiences, and celebrity fans and anti-fans, do not engage with celebrities in reality TV in quite the same way as for other entertainment. The placement of reality television as popular entertainment can work against a positive emotional engagement with celebrities performing as themselves, instead sometimes widening a point of negative engagement and providing a space for celebrity anti-fans to express extreme views, especially through social media.

Given that reality television crosses boundaries between fact and entertainment, the dividing line for celebrities and ordinary people in the public–private sphere is blurred. Competitive reality offers ordinary people a chance to become a celebrity, gaining notoriety during a series and capitalizing on a brief moment in the spotlight. Commonly referred to as 'fifteen minutes of fame', a reference to a saying by the pop artist Andy Warhol, ordinary people in competitive reality occupy an unenviable position of being neither thought of as ordinary, nor as a celebrity. They are celebrity wannabes. One viewer described it in 2000 as *'Big Brother* watching you syndrome' (male viewer aged 18–34).

Structured reality, or reality soaps, offer a chance for professional reality performers to generate a career as reality TV stars. Performers in *Keeping Up with the Kardashians*, *Here Comes Honey Boo Boo* or *The Only Way is Essex* are what Charlie Brooker (2012) describes as authorized media hate figures. These are performers who aspire to be hated by millions, and actively work at gaining negative attention as notorious figures in the media (see next chapter). This is a bit like the pantomime performances of 'nasty' judges in talent formats who regularly court boos from the live audience. People actively style themselves as celebrity wannabes no matter what the cost. Brooker's description of media hate figures signifies the type of performer common to structured reality series, often aimed at younger audiences and social media users.

Celebrity reality formats include a range of celebrities, such as singers, actors, musicians, sports professionals, former reality TV contestants and reality TV stars, who showcase their talents and personalities. These celebrities re-boot their careers, riding a wave of media attention in a short-lived moment as a reality TV celebrity. A common way of describing celebrity contestants in reality formats is D-list, or even Z-list celebrities. In actual fact, some talent formats contain big name celebrities that the public get behind and vote for, positively engaging with a celebrity as they experience being a ballroom dancer, or being a chef, in warm reality shows. But, this reference to D-list celebrities signals how the entertainment market over the past decade has become saturated with celebrities vying to get on series such as *I'm a Celebrity ...* or *Celebrity Big Brother*, seemingly just to be in the public eye. It is the short time span associated with the throwaway cultural value of reality TV that is the killer blow to a celebrity performance in this genre. One viewer explained celebrity reality TV as a place where celebrities go to die: 'I mean that is really fascinating, because I mean that's basically where they just die quite slowly and rather sadly' (39-year-old male health psychologist).

In terms of emotional economics, there is a market in negative emotions for celebrity wannabes and celebrities in reality TV. This is a somewhat different situation to the emotional engagement of audiences with performers in reality talent formats such as *Got to Dance* where viewers are moved by an emotional truth in a young teenager's dream of being a professional dancer. *American Idol* performers are another category of professional reality contestants, people who knowingly play the fame game. Mama June in *Here Comes Honey Boo Boo* knew what she was doing when she uploaded a clip of her daughter as a 'red neck' reality TV star to YouTube. After her daughter's appearance in a reality series about child beauty pageants, it was only a matter of time and social media attention before the child Honey Boo Boo was offered her own series on TLC, reportedly earning in the range of 40,000 US dollars per series. The type of emotional engagement with Honey Boo Boo is an experience of memorable moments along the lines of 'would you look at that!' If anything, it is a tourism experience of a dramatized 'red neck' family in the Midwest that bears little relation to people's real experiences of living in America. It is a faux reality celebrity experience.

For celebrities, it is a risky business appearing in a reality format. The emotional economics at work in celebrity reality creates a market of desperation. If reality TV is where celebrities go to die then the public witness their slow demise. It is a sad performance of the self for some celebrities in reality entertainment. The value of celebrity as a special place in society and culture is derided in formats like *I'm a Celebrity* ... For example, the performance of celebrity within the media industry and public relations is deconstructed in post-rehab reality show *Lindsay* (OWN 2014–), following the Hollywood actress Lindsay Lohan and her troubled life in and out of rehab. The series sells an emotional experience of a celebrity as she struggles to overcome addiction and deal with her personal life in the public scrutiny of the world's media. But, the experience of Lohan in a reality TV show is not perceived as emotionally authentic. Critics accuse her of using reality TV to reboot her career, a strategy that both works in the sense of media attention and front-page tabloid news, and backfires in the sense of the sad performance of a celebrity so low as to star in a post-rehab reality show.

Chris Rojek (2001) makes a distinction between celebrities, who have a skill of some kind as a professional performer, and celetoids, who do not have such skills. A celebrity is the 'attribution of glamorous or notorious status to an individual within the public sphere' (Rojek 2001: 9). Celebrity equals an impact on public consciousness; it involves 'the scheduling of emotions', the 'presentation of the self in interpersonal relations and impression management', and it permeates everyday life (ibid.). Celebrities are cultural fabrications that involve a host of professionals and amateurs, consumers and publics, in a 'chain of attraction' (2001: 10). Media is at the centre of a celebrity culture, and relates to the 'mysterious tenacity of celebrity power and the peculiar fragility of celebrity presence' (2001: 14). In contrast, a celetoid is a form of attributed celebrity, their glamour and notoriety are compressed and short-lived. Celetoids are 'accessories of culture' (2001: 16). Another type of attributed celebrity are celeactors, similar to a satirical form of celetoids, often involving professional comedians. In the case of celebrity wannabes, this category of performer could be an example of celetoids, an accessory to pick up and discard as fashion dictates. Professional reality performers of the kind that are media hate figures could also be celetoids in that the chain of attraction is short; they also seem to satirize themselves in a knowing performance as a hate figure. As for celebrities, some manage to retain their presence but many lose their power as celebrities and become sad figures, Z-list celebrities who do the circuit of competitive reality.

Misha Kavka (2012) argues that in the history of reality television, the rise of celebrity-based formats, and the notoriety of professional reality contestants, represents a new wave of the genre in the 2000s. In the 1990s the notion of celebrities and ordinary people as celebrities was a minor element in the genre as a whole. When designing a survey on British reality TV in 2000, no sub-category of celebrity programmes appeared on a list of titles. Questions related to a range of sub-categories of reality television, including police/crime, emergency services, motorways/driving, hospitals/doctors, building/DIY, homes and gardens, holidays/travel, survival, places, marriage/relationships, pet shows and people programmes. The list of categories was based on a scheduling, ratings and genre analysis in the year 2000. The list reflects the fact that celebrities were not a major feature of the genre at this juncture in time. It would be impossible to design a survey today without several sub-categories relating to ordinary people as celebrities and celebrities as ordinary people.

The timing of the survey is suggestive of a shift in audience preferences for competitive reality, in particular with younger viewers, the key advertising market for competitive reality formats. When asked what they liked about reality TV in 2000, all adult respondents (8,216, aged 16–65+) claimed they liked up-to-the-minute stories (74 per cent), information (75 per cent), stories caught on camera (68 per cent), presenters (60 per cent), members of the public (58 per cent) and animals (60 per cent). Respondents least liked intrusive cameras (19 per cent), arguments and disagreements (38 per cent), and looking into other people's lives (46 per cent). Younger viewers were more interested in the nosey side of reality TV. Of those respondents that liked intrusive cameras 40 per cent were aged 16–24, looking into other people's lives 64 per cent aged 16–24, and arguments and disagreements 60 per cent aged 16–24. In a representative survey of 937 respondents aged 4–15 years old (2000, UK), 75 per cent of 10–15 year olds liked stories caught on camera, 44 per cent of 10–15 year olds liked looking into other people's lives, 50 per cent liked arguments and disagreements, and 35 per cent liked intrusive cameras. Compare these figures to 50 per cent of 10–15 year olds who liked information in reality programmes. We can see the early signs of a shift from infotainment to entertainment within the target younger audience for reality television.

In focus groups at this time, younger viewers reflected on the impact of *Big Brother* and the rise in competitive reality formats that showed ordinary people both being themselves and competing to win, triggering a chain of attraction across media and the public eye. 'They basically, like, went in only known by their friends and they came out really famous' (12–15-year-old male viewer). Such a quote demonstrates the democratization of the fame argument put forward by the media industry in their promotion of this new breed of reality star. A 12–15-year-old female viewer reflected on the cult of *Big Brother*:

> [A]ll the people who were in the house, they are going to be famous forever now because *Big Brother* was such a cult programme, and they're, like, still doing reruns of it and they've made videos and they've made games and ... they will be famous for a long time cos everyone will know what *Big Brother* is.

In hindsight, this viewer's comment highlights how the format became more well known than the people in it. The spiral of reality television series, reruns, promotions and games worked against the cultural value of participants who became caught up in the cult and were unable to foster a career beyond the moment of initial impact on the public consciousness. Their fame was cut short because of the format's regeneration with contestants for each season. As Douglas Wood, Head of Audience Research at Shine Group notes: '*Big Brother* isn't there to make stars, it is there to entertain the audience.'

Few viewers in the study of 2000 believed that participants in *Big Brother* could be famous in the same way as other celebrities.

For example, these 12–15-year-old female viewers reflected on the tricky distinction between celebrities and ordinary people:

Fay: All celebrities are real people at the end of the day, really. You've just got to get there somehow and that's the way they've got there. I think it's quite good, you know. I would do it just to be on TV afterwards!

Laura: You can't really say 'real people being celebrities' cos celebrities are real people ... they just become well known. Or maybe not even well known. I don't think the *Big Brother* people are well known, I think they're known. Someone who's well known is someone like Madonna. They're just known. Not everyone would ... if you saw them walking down the street, not everyone would know who they are. Someone well known would walk down the street and everyone would know who it is. So, I don't know ... they're just known.

The distinction of being 'well known' and 'just known' high-lights the different cultural value of celebrities and reality TV contestants.

A typical phrase in audience discussions of ordinary people as celebrities was 'where are they now?' For example, two female viewers (aged 18–34) commented on the winner of *Big Brother* UK in 2000:

Vicki: I don't think it takes a lot to make anybody a celebrity in this country.

Isabel: It's short term, isn't it? He's only going to be a celebrity like, initially after the programme ... after a year's time, people will not know him.

Sandra: It'll be like that programme, *Where Are They Now?* ...

In another example, these male viewers (aged 18–34) noted:

Mike: One minute they're nothing – not nothing but, one minute they're like normal working class, the next they're on national TV! ... Every one knew on the *Big Brother* they were going to make it ...

> Eric: Yeah, but everybody has to be discovered at some stage.
>
> Paul: Yeah, but in a year's time, they'll go *Big Brother* who?

The democratization of fame is a hollow claim within competitive reality formats.

Another issue that arises in discussions of reality television is the claim that audiences see themselves reflected in the journey of reality participants – 'one minute they're nothing' and 'the next they're on national TV!' It is certainly the case that performers in competitive reality are formerly the audience. These people are aspiring professional reality contestants, responding to casting calls, going repeatedly to auditions, signing with agencies, so that they can tailor their performances towards what they assume producers and the public wants. And some of the contestants who make it to the top ten, or semi-finals, in talent shows are repeat performers, who may have auditioned several times before finally hitting the right level of performance and emotional investment that the series producers and judges are looking for. So strong is this trend that reality casting agents scour shopping malls and bars looking for people who are not professional reality contestants, hoping for a more authentic performance of the self in certain shows (see Mayer 2011).

The performer as former audience does not stand in for the audience at large. If anything, reality celebrity experiences put some audiences off the idea of celebrity in a genre such as this. Formats consultant Julie Donovan (2013) notes: '[T]he audience create celebrities. They are completely involved in the process. Audiences create this minor celebrity by voting for them to win, and then, when they turn into a celebrity, viewers often discard them.' This woman explained: 'Personally, it just infuriates me that people can be that stupid … so, no I wouldn't. And I don't care how much they were paying me, I wouldn't embarrass myself like that' (female viewer aged 18–34). Audiences distance themselves from celebrity wannabes, thinking 'thank god I am not like that' (see Skeggs and Wood 2012).

In many ways the genre has widened the point of consumption for celebrities and professional reality TV contestants, but it has also narrowed the point of identification with these people. In a representative survey of 4,516 respondents aged 16–65+ (UK, 2003) only 30 per cent of respondents claimed celebrities were treated fairly by reality programme makers and 45 per cent didn't know if they were treated fairly or not. Less than one-third of the sample said it was very important that celebrities were treated fairly in reality TV. It is not so much that viewers have lost their belief in fair treatment as a moral principle, but that they hold in low esteem celebrities who choose to compete in reality formats. Something similar can be said of attitudes towards fair treatment of the value of people in general in competitive reality. Only 35 per cent of the sample agreed with the statement 'I think young children are treated fairly in reality programmes', 36 per cent of the sample agreed with this statement for women, 36 per cent for men and 31 per cent for teenagers participating in reality programmes.

TV critics speak of reality TV desperados in their reviews of the latest reality talent formats or structured reality shows. Perhaps this is the point of emotional engagement for audiences, the desperation in people who will stop at nothing to be famous. These viewers reflected on the celebrity cult in reality TV:

Sarah: Well, we all have things that we are living for, a dream. And they're kind of just exposing them on TV ... I don't know. I suppose it's like a mad dream that they kind of try and achieve through telly. You know, becoming famous (30-year-old female multimedia developer).

Carl: Yeah, the celebrity cult, it's mental actually (35-year-old male printer).

Here, then, reality TV becomes a spectacle for the mad dream of celebrity.

The idea of human experience in a mediated society becomes caught up in reality talent formats that drive a cult of celebrity. *The Hunger Games* novels by Suzanne Collins satirize this dystopian vision of a future reality TV landscape. One viewer joked of celebrities in reality TV: 'load a gun to mow them down' (34-year-old male sales worker). The genre becomes a space for celebrity anti-fans to communicate extreme expressions, particularly in social media (see next chapter). The genre can be a negative space for celebrity culture. This is part of the reason why talent formats have experienced a downturn in ratings, especially with younger viewers. 'I am getting fed up with the whole celebrity thing ... I find myself sort of thinking, "what am I doing here?"' (32-year-old female personal assistant).

CONCLUSION

Reality TV is at the forefront of an experience economy where consumer engagement, performance and experience are centre stage. From a marketing perspective, and the business trends in an experience economy or affective economics, reality TV content draws on narrative, drama and direct experience of life. This mix of fact and drama helps to create individual and collective cultural experiences that people will pay for again and again. Reality formats such as *American Idol* contain tight interactivity in the form of public auditions, voting or social media, which functions as a driver to increase audience investment in the live event as it builds momentum through the season and is rolled out around the world. Reality TV producers and participants work on enhancing drama, tragedy and comedy, rehearsing and scripting certain types of characters and their emotional journey. The 'active-style dialogue' of reality performances works alongside vocal and physical performances, creating emotional hubs for audience engagement.

Similar to the sports industry, passion play has become a major feature of the genre and its positioning in an experience or emotional economy. Reality TV makes consumers, audiences and publics visible and audible, through participating in shows as live crowds, in auditions, as contestants, as themselves, through voting, or making and sharing content for social media, and through gossiping, people watching and public debate. In terms of making the cult of celebrity visible to audiences, it highlights two issues. The first is that the experience of becoming a reality TV celebrity opened the floodgates to a new breed of professional reality contestant. Audiences do not perceive these people as ordinary, but instead driven by a desire to be famous at any cost. The second issue is that celebrity formats offer a point of identification with famous people who want to court public attention. However, the celebrity status of these contestants can also be devalued as they became part of the commercialization of the genre. The immersive, interactive elements of reality TV suggest a widening point of consumption for performance, celebrity and social relations. But this commercial driver can also narrow the point of identification with the experiences of ordinary people as celebrities and celebrities as ordinary people within the throwaway culture of reality TV.

5

REALITY AND SPORTS ENTERTAINMENT

Good match, love to hate you.

(Anti-fan at after-party)

Professional wrestling has a special place in popular culture as over-the-top sports entertainment with talk of fixed fights and rowdy crowds. When you go to a live wrestling match it is easy to see why pro wrestling has a reputation; there are wrestlers in bright costumes, capes and masks, performing heroes and villains to a crowd of fans and anti-fans who cheer and boo for these stars of the wrestling ring. With historical roots in Victorian carnivals, Mexican *lucha libre*, or British and American freestyle wrestling, this kind of contemporary wrestling is described as sports entertainment to signal its spectacular nature. In turn, reality television is commonly talked about as popular entertainment, full of staged moments, peopled by wannabe celebrities and popular with the masses. When you watch reality TV it is easy to see why the genre has this kind of reputation; there are celebrities and participants in staged settings from studios to jungles, performing

Figure 5.1 Wrestling as spectacle of excess. Photograph: Fredrik Schoug.

meta versions of themselves to audiences, live crowds, fans and anti-fans, who chat, vote and tweet for the people they love and love to hate. With historical roots in variety theatre, radio and television fictional and factual programming, reality TV is usually described as an entertainment genre.

This chapter draws on sports entertainment to illustrate how to understand reality entertainment as a cultural performance. A key point of departure is Roland Barthes' (1957, 1972) seminal writing on the world of wrestling as a spectacle of excess. Jeffrey Sconce's research on the show *Celebrity Boxing* on Fox (2002, USA) in America also examines the spectacle and textual play of producers, participants and viewers of reality entertainment (2004). Both works are richly suggestive for research on sports and reality entertainment. The empirical research in this chapter draws on qualitative methods, from interviews, focus groups and participant observation of professional wrestling live events, and reality television, as pre-recorded and live content for cross-media. This empirical research with professional wrestlers, promoters, producers, crowds, audiences, fans and anti-fans allows for an exploration of spectacle, play and passion in these infamous examples of popular culture.

SPORTS ENTERTAINMENT

Picture pro wrestling and probably the first thing to come to mind is aggressive, over-the-top American wrestling associated with World Wrestling Entertainment (WWE, formerly World Wrestling Federation). This is wrestling on cable television and pay-per-view live events, with larger than life characters in serialized soap opera narratives, where there is much pre-match banter and short brutal matches. An alternative style of wrestling is Mexican *lucha libre*, originally based on American wrestling from the 1930s. This more athletic version of pro wrestling involves brightly coloured costumes and masks. 'In U.S. wrestling, they talk for 10 minutes and wrestle for one. In lucha libre, it's very intense athletics for 20 or 30 minutes' (Levi cited in Hawley 2009). Whilst American and Mexican wrestling are markedly different in style, both share national popularity as sports entertainment, featuring not only in live sporting events and televised matches, but in other cultural forms such as films, street art, graphic novels, toys, T-shirts and computer games.

In Scott Beekman's history of wrestling in America, he points out that 'pro wrestling did not always resemble sports entertainment' (Beekman 2006: x). Grappling is an ancient form of sports and has a long history in various civilizations. It is associated with the beginnings of sporting culture in the ancient Near East, with recordings of wrestling bouts in Eygpt, Greece and Rome. Wrestling was part of early sporting cultures during the Renaissance period and was 'probably the most popular spectator sport in Northern Europe' (Beekman 2006: 4). In Renaissance England, there were local variations of wrestling, including violent tavern matches that could involve heavy drinking and rowdy outbursts by the crowds; one style from Lancashire called catch-as-catch-can was particularly barbaric and eventually became the influence for American wrestling during the nineteenth century (Beekman 2006: 5–7).

The historical background to sports entertainment includes nineteenth-century carnivals and travelling attractions in Britain and America, where travellers would pit themselves against local strong men in physical, lengthy and violent fights. Maguire (2005: 156) notes that some time around the early 1900s professional wrestling transformed from sports competition to orchestrated entertainment, thus giving rise to the fakery claims that have framed this kind of wrestling. Beekman argues that before the First World War, national and world champion wrestlers managed a certain level of control over their careers, but after the war wrestling promoters took control and the balance of power shifted from individual athletes to the wrestling business: 'the promoters recognised that pre-determined finishes kept fans interested in their product and left wrestlers at their mercy' (2006: x).

Pro wrestling 'should be viewed as an important entertainment form central to the growth of new media technologies over the last half century' (Beekman 2006: ix). Wrestling was significant to the rise of network television in the post-war era in America, and again featured as popular content for the cable market during the 1980s. The key figure behind sports entertainment in America, Vince McMahon, redefined professional wrestling as 'sports entertainment'. Although a redefinition resulted in criticism and legal battles with other promoters, this blatantly commercial move paid off. McMahon floated WWE on the US stock exchange in 2001; *Business Week* ranked it as the third best small company in America with annual revenues that year of $456 million dollars. Even though pro wrestling is not at its peak of the 1980s, WWE is the world's leading pay-per-view provider, schedules weekly fights on primetime cable television, and has a wealth of syndicated shows (Beekman 2006: 143).

According to Heather Levi in her book *The World of Lucha Libre* (2008), pro wrestling is a cultural performance in regions as diverse as Mexico, the USA, Japan and Europe. Levi is inspired by an anthropology of performance (see Richard Schechner 1977, 2004, and Victor Turner 1986, amongst others). She explains that Mexican wrestling combines aerial moves, holds, gymnastics and mixed martial arts, but its 'raison d'etre is to offer audiences a spectacular performance' (Levi 1998: 277). Rather than see this contradiction as a problem of legitimacy within wrestling as sports *or* entertainment, Levi argues that pro wrestling in Mexico should be understood as staging contradictions; it 'occupies a space between sport, ritual and theatre and is thus capable of drawing its power from all of those genres' (2008: 6).

The work in this chapter uses a definition of pro wrestling as cultural performance. The focus here is on live performance of pro wrestling events. Set within the context of global pro wrestling, this research illuminates a local interpretation of a transnational sports entertainment. What follows in the next section is an analysis of empirical materials drawn from interviews and participant observations of promoters, professional wrestlers and live crowds of matches in southern Sweden during 2012–14. As background to the analysis, this style of pro wrestling combines acrobatic, aerial moves and colourful characters, and hardcore matches with props and stunts. The combination of American WWE and *lucha libre*-style wrestling makes for a mixed mode event, with serious and comedy matches lasting around 15 minutes each in an overall event of three hours. The live crowds resemble those at a rock gig; there are fans, families, children wearing costumes of their favourite wrestling stars, groups of male and female friends on a good night

Figure 5.2 Hushing mime (Dan Ahtola). Photograph: Michael Rübsamen.

out and curious newcomers. There are more men than women, although both are vocal. The music is hard rock, and the dress sense tends to be rockabilly with an edge. This is a distinctly regional adaptation of a worldwide sports entertainment, showcasing local knowledge by event management, Nordic wrestlers and their fans, and nightlife in southern Sweden and Denmark. At one event, fans of local wrestler The Mime offered wrestling cupcakes to the crowd. The wrestling cupcakes signify the playful practices at work in this kind of local cultural performance.

SPECTACULAR ENTERTAINMENT

Seen as popular culture for working-class crowds, sports entertainment is much maligned in the press and general public. 'Professional wrestling is often derided as simplistic, contrived and full of gratuitous violence' (Levi 2008: 5). Pro wrestling is all of these things – simple in the characters of good and evil, contrived in the predetermined endings to matches, and full of violent acts, usually between men, in unreconstructed performances of masculinity and physical power. In the case of *lucha libre* and this research, there are also matches involving women and transsexual and transgender performers (see Levi 2008). Rather than argue against these criticisms, a good promoter knows these elements are selling points. Promoter and pro wrestler Dan Ahtola established wrestling in southern Sweden in the early 2000s. He describes the essence of sports entertainment: 'wrestling is acrobatic, violent entertainment. Low brow culture' (2012). For example, a popular local wrestling character is a drunken clown, who drinks too many beers from fans, and pokes fun at his opponents.

In Roland Barthes' (1972: 15) work on the world of wrestling, he describes it as popular drama: 'a light without shadow generates emotion without reserve'. A pro wrestler said: 'from the moment the wrestlers enter the ring, the crowd can ask is he a hero or villain, it is that easy'. At an event in 2012, a male fan sitting in the front row explained how to follow what was happening: 'Just go with the flow. If they chant you chant, and if you don't want to chant you boo.' Ahtola (2012) explained what he hoped to achieve in promoting this event:

> For a few hours, the world outside doesn't matter, you can forget about it. This is all that matters right now, good versus evil, solve conflicts with violence, simple drama. I think that is why people like it so much. It is black and white, good versus evil, nothing in between. In the real world nothing like that exists.

When speaking with first-time participants at an event, people had mixed expectations of pro wrestling. One male rookie said he was 'hoping for good entertainment, a lot of action, a lot of screaming. Hoping for some fun' (December 2012). A male fan reflected on his first time: 'I thought this is like going to the theatre. But, when I got here the first time I loved it. I had a great time' (December 2012). By theatre, this fan means a middle-class live cultural performance where there are etiquette rules. What he loved about this promoter's matches, what made him come back again and again, was precisely the 'emotion without reserve' (Barthes 1972: 15).

The girlfriend of a pro-wrestler explained her first reaction to live sports entertainment:

> Wrestling? I was expecting something less. But it has a big impact. It's more dramatic than I thought. You have the music, you see up close, you hear a lot of the bounces, you really hear the sound. It has quite an impact.
>
> (December 2012)

When her boyfriend came crashing down on the front row seats during his match, the crowd really heard the bounce and felt the impact. There was a collective rush to get out of the way, and mass screaming by the 300-plus audience at the venue. In a previous match, this pro wrestler was rushed to hospital for stitches after the event such was the impact of his dramatic aerial moves outside the ring. These are big performances that generate a frenetic experience. As Ahtola (2012) notes, 'this is chaos'.

Barthes (1972: 15) said of the wrestling public, 'what matters is not what it thinks but what it sees'. Sports scholars have noted how live events can create a heightened affective form of communication between an athlete and the crowd (see Boyle and

Haynes 2009). Modes of engagement that are about how we feel and what we see are paramount in live pro wrestling matches. The point is not to rationalize this kind of engagement, nor to dismiss it as unthinking reactions to low-brow culture. According to Barthes (1972: 25) wrestling is 'a pure and full signification' where there is a 'perfect intelligibility of reality', a 'real understanding of things'. As summed up by one pro wrestler: 'You can spoil a lot of things by intellectualizing them.'

When Barthes (1972: 16) commented on the crowd for wrestling in 1950s Europe, he explained the power of such experiences as 'each moment imposes the total knowledge of passion'. Barthes is referring to the participatory spectatorship of live sporting events. In this context, a 'total knowledge of passion' refers to the collective energy of the crowd as they physically react to each moment of a match. Whilst much has changed in pro wrestling, with increased commercialization and the televising of sports entertainment, his comment is still relevant to live matches of the kind researched here. The knowledge of the crowd is about a live sporting drama. Although television viewers and fans have knowledge of pro wrestling skills, and knowledge of this transnational genre as it works in America, Mexico and Europe, this is not the implicit knowledge that Barthes connects with passion at a live event. The moment-by-moment live performance that creates a total knowledge of passion is experienced by the crowd like an electric current.

Ahtola (2012) described his first live match: 'I felt so much in the moment. It totally captured me. I couldn't think of anything else.' This experience was to start his passion for pro wrestling, inspiring him to train, perform and promote wrestling in his home country. This is passionate engagement of the kind that Barthes describes as unique to the world of wrestling. When asked to describe their experience at these live events, people used words like excitement, adrenalin kick, amazement, drama – 'you can't expect much more than this' (male rookie, December 2012). When culture captures you in this way it is a total knowledge of passion. 'I want people to experience the same thing I experienced the first time, you can't control your emotions. You hear someone screaming and then you realize it is you' (Ahtola 2012).

Wrestling crowds are reacting to professionals, who are in turn working for promoters who hold enormous power in the sports entertainment industry. As a good promoter Ahtola understands the crowd is crucial to shaping an emotional structure to the event. His knowledge of pro wrestling as live performance is clear to see when attending events he has managed and ones promoted by other professionals. The structuring of an event so that crowds 'pop', that is to say physically and emotional engage with a match, takes detailed knowledge of the profession of wrestling, skills in event management and hard-won knowledge as a pro wrestler of the passion of fans and anti-fans, screaming until their voices are hoarse.

Critics of sports entertainment claim that violence and emotional expression of the kind experienced at a pro wrestling event can be damaging. This spectacle of excess is not part of a civilizing process. But, as Norbert Elias and Eric Dunning (1986) note in their book *The Quest for Excitement: Sport and Leisure in the Civilizing Process*, letting go of emotional control is not something to be viewed as only negative. They argue that sporting events are stage managed to produce a balance of tension and excitement. In the case of sports entertainment, promoters and pro wrestlers create controlled chaos. They draw on different skills related to the craft of wrestling, such as acrobatic moves; careful use of the space inside and outside of the ring, including pre-match and post-match entrances and exits; choice of characters, costumes and props, such as heroes and heels (also called babyfaces); interaction with non-wrestlers, including the referees and stage crew; and audience management, such as amplifying the noise of the crowd, inciting chants and boos.

And audiences create controlled chaos. They draw on skills related to being a member of a crowd; cautious use of the space outside the ring, standing at the back, sitting at the front where the action takes place, being at the side to greet the wrestlers entering the ring; playing certain roles, such as chanting or booing for heroes and heels; using props, like offering a wrestler a beer; and interaction with the wrestlers during a match through noise amplification, attention to the action and participation as fans and anti-fans. Henricks noted 'fans go for "the action" and it is the performer who can "put on a show" and convince the audience of the hazards of his art that is most popular' (Henricks

1974: 185). We can also say fans and anti-fans put on a show – they are revelling in controlled chaos.

Research on fans and anti-fans (see Gray 2003 amongst others) has emphasized similar modes of engagement by people who love and love to hate media content, or celebrities. Liz Giuffre (2014) researched music anti-fans at live events. She argues that spontaneous responses by anti-fans can be constructive and are a normal process of engagement with live music. She gives an example of anti-fans voting with their feet to try to change the musical direction of a DJ. A similar process of engagement takes place with fans and anti-fans at live matches. In pro wrestling the crowd is made up of fans and anti-fans because this is the point of the sporting drama, to chant or boo for heroes and heels. Being an anti-fan is constructive; the wrestlers as heels need excessive and negative emotions, they feed off the energy of anti-fans. And when a heel enters the ring, or performs a low move, the crowd is being anti-fans en masse, not just a few people in the front row. It is one of the key attractions of a live match that there can be a collective, scripted and spontaneous negative engagement with a heel, what Barthes (1972: 24) calls unrestrained contempt. Anti-fan engagement is vocal, energizing and fun.

Arlie Hochschild (2003) has written extensively about the commercialization of intimate life where emotions are something to control through feeling rules, or to exploit through emotional economics. The rules and norms of how we feel, or the ways we choose to express our feelings, are governed by a 'larger social context in which some expressions are custom scarce and others abundant' (2003: 83). Hochschild (2003: 84) notes:

> [I]n a commercialised society, positive expression is more 'inflated' than expression, say, of envy, anger and resentment. There are more phony dollars in circulation. So a slight expression of anger is trusted to respond to felt anger in a way not generally true for an expression of liking. Expressions of anger are more 'serious' and more likely to be sensed as 'true.'

The opposite works in sports entertainment. Hot passions rule, like rage, suffering or defeat. Physical violence is always used as conflict resolution. If violence and anger are custom scarce in a market of expressions, then they are in abundance in the entertainment market. And these expressions are not generally true, but phony expressions circulated by pro wrestlers and crowds.

For example, a group of young men at an event (June 2013) switched into character as frenetic fans and anti-fans. Positioned to interact with wrestlers as they walked past the crowd, these men screamed abuse, one getting right in the face of a heel; wrestler and anti-fan showing their hatred for each other, giving the finger and then laughing at the sheer fun of it all. A woman in her sixties, sitting with her husband, stood up and booed the heel, jumping to the front, screaming at the top of her voice for her hero. After the match, she politely greeted her favourite wrestler as they became part of the crowd – neither fan nor wrestler was in character now. Dan Ahtola said: 'We want people to jump up and down, scream, act like they wouldn't normally do outside because this is another world. They can be someone else in another world' (Ahtola 2013). Here, hot passions are performed in a managed and safe spectacle of excess.

FAKING IT, SMART FANS AND MARKS

Roland Barthes commented on passion in wrestling: '[I]t no longer matters whether the passion is genuine or not. What the public wants is the image of passion, not passion itself' (1972: 18). The image of passion that Barthes talks about is the performance by wrestlers, where heroes and heels go head to head in a dramatic match. As wrestling became popular in the 1980s as the World Wrestling Federation, now WWE, the sports entertainment industry used an image of passion as a driver in a commercialized society. Other areas of sports, such as football, also became adept at using the passion of supporters and fans to make money, leading to an increased commercialization of sports as global media and leisure industries. Alongside the emotional economics at work in sports entertainment, there is the added dimension that professional wrestling is caught up in fakery claims due to its predetermined finishes. If wrestlers are faking it, then the idea of an image of passion from Barthes becomes altered in this commercial context. In contemporary sports entertainment the performances of pro wrestlers are being sold to consumers. This means that the value of pro wrestling is bound up with physical, emotional and violent performances of matches, rather than a competitive sporting event.

An image of passion is not limited to pro wrestlers but also includes a spectacle of passionate fans and anti-fans. These images of passionate crowds are what Rowe and Baker (2012) call hyperbolic expressions of fandom. For example, football fans are co-opted by the sports industry to promote an image of passion. At football fan events, coordinated with live matches for the 2012 World Cup, fans dressed up in elaborate costumes, wanting to be caught on camera in a co-performance between the media and the public (Becker, Kautsky and Widholm 2014). When wrestling fans and anti-fans are used as an image of passion in promotional material and news coverage of events they are often a figure of fun, exploited by the industry for their support of a fake sport. The referee is a joke, rules are meant to be broken, foul play is to be expected. Wrestling fans and anti-fans are often pictured wearing costumes or masks, screaming and chanting; they are part of the serialized soap opera narrative of sports entertainment.

In wrestling terms, audiences are smart fans and marks. This is carny talk for people who are easily deceived and open to exploitation (Kerrick 1980). A smart fan is someone who thinks they know how pro wrestling works, gathering knowledge on the various schools of wrestling, acrobatics, mixed martial arts, knowing the back stories to pro wrestling characters. At a match, smart fans are an example of hyperbolic expressions of fandom, and promoters want these fans ringside, generating pre-match and live match excitement. Marks are the rest of the crowd who can be manipulated to create an exciting match. A wrestler explained: 'To us you are all marks. You are all part of the show. You don't really know why you are reacting and you are reacting the way we want you to' (December 2012).

Peter Lunt and Paul Stenner (2005) analysed talkshows like *Jerry Springer* (USA, 1991–), similarly accused of faking it, and used as an example of the commercialization of excess. They argue that assumptions regarding the fakery of the people on display miss the point that talkshows invite audiences to controlled chaos. For Lunt and Stenner, a low-brow talkshow like *Springer* highlights the significance of scripting and ritual elements of communication and spontaneity. People at live wrestling matches in this case study are paying for the chance to spontaneously express themselves within the scripting and ritual elements of an event. Similar to Levi's (2008) research in *lucha libre*, what the empirical evidence suggests is that crowds willingly engage with the contradictory elements of drama, ritual and sport. There is an image of passion – the performance within a scripted event – and an expression of passion – the ritual and sporting elements within a spontaneous live event.

Levi (2008) points out that whilst critics of *lucha libre* decry its scripted elements, Mexican wrestlers deny fakery charges, claiming their style of wrestling derives from the circus and sports. According to Beekman (2006), WWE wrestlers face 'fantastically dangerous working environments' with 'serious injuries and shortened careers' as a result of these kinds of brutal matches (2006: 142). 'A frighteningly high percentage of wrestlers die before the age of forty because of hardcore matches and outrageous stunts and gimmicks'; caught in a vicious circle of medication for injuries sustained in training and the ring, pro wrestlers often die young from accidents, drug overdose or alcohol addiction (Beekman ibid.). In a study of American pro wrestlers Tyson Smith (2008) points to the contradictions at work in the physical and emotional performance of professionals. Often, what looks like a relatively painless manoeuvre is actually painful for wrestlers; conversely when wrestlers show pain they are often performing rather than feeling pain. Tyson Smith argues that pro wrestlers are emotional co-workers, managing high levels of pain and performing at the same time as a team: '[T]he performance is an enactment of a duel between two or more fighters who are, in actuality, colluding with one another' (2008: 158).

As a wrestler Dan Ahtola (2013) explains: 'Fake is a term I never use, because basically it isn't. Is the punch fake, the blood fake, the falling onto the floor fake? Everything hurts.' If the match is fake, and still 'everything hurts', then this creates a contradictory experience for the audience. One response to this issue is to say audiences suspend their disbelief, just as they would in magical entertainment (see Levi 2008 amongst others). However, magicians argue they take their audience deftly by the hand and invite them to experience a sense of wonder. This experience is more along the lines of a will to believe, something William James (1896) associated with religious and psychic matters. In research on audiences for the mentalist Derren Brown, people did not suspend their disbelief, just turning off their scepticism like the flick of a switch. Rather, audiences entered into a co-performance with Brown who orchestrated a complex set of cognitive, emotional and physical responses to this kind of psychological entertainment (Hill 2011).

Wrestlers and their audiences similarly enter into a knowing relationship, co-creating a cultural performance. It is worth unpacking what is happening when people react to something that appears so fake. First, crowds for sports entertainment are following a certain script established by promoters and wrestlers. For example, the music used to accompany the entrance of wrestlers can cue the crowd to burst into activity, and signal the kind of battle on offer – the *Rocky* theme tune (1976, director John G. Avildsen) tells a story of the underdog. The serialized narratives that accompany matches are also cues, with narrative arcs built up over time concerning epic battles or long-term rivalries, told through previous events and promotional media.

Crowds at live events follow certain practices for expressing themselves in controlled chaos. 'Everything is allowed, except throwing things, or getting into the ring' (Ahtola 2013). By everything Ahtola means strong expressions and crazy behaviour that fits with a pro wrestling event. Crowds do not act like mobs. Promoters and pro wrestlers control how crowds interact within the venue. A criticism of journalists covering crowds for pro wrestling is that they believe jokes made by fans that wrestling incites them to violence. Rivalry between fans is encouraged by wrestlers during a match, but rivalry outside of an event would be rare indeed. At this venue there is a post-match party where wrestlers, fans and anti-fans mingle as they might at a music gig after the main event is over.

Ahtola (2013) commented:

> My wife was watching some matches, she knows everyone I am fighting and training with, she is friends with them, but during the match she is screaming for his opponent, kick his head in, make him bleed. She is completely honest, it doesn't sound fake. She sounds completely mad. Afterwards, 'that was a good match, are you OK?', did it hurt?' It is something I really don't see in her that often.

There is a structured spontaneity to the cultural performance of pro wrestling. As a wrestler Ahtola (2013) knows how to work with his audience:

> They are responding to what we do, we are responding to what they do. If they are quiet, you have to create a situation where they need to scream or clap. It is not about doing a fancy move. That is cheap. I try to create a situation that makes them react. But if they are constantly loud that is like the perfect wave for the surfer.

This idea of riding the perfect wave sums up the feeling of being part of a live match. 'We are totally dependent on what the audience is doing. I don't think they know how important they are' (Ahtola 2012). Audiences do know how important they are: 'I felt excited. The crowd did it all, the energy and feeling' (wrestling fan, December 2012).

Nowhere is this co-performance of emotional and physical excess more apparent than when wrestlers jump into crowds. The ring is a sacred space, including the perimeter where interaction with the crowd takes place in the form of fights that spill over onto the first row seats. It is where the power lies: the power of the promoters in staging a spectacle, the powerful performances of wrestlers inside and outside this space, and the power of crowds to act out their feelings. Ahtola (2012) describes why the ring is so important to the drama and ritual of this sport:

> What we want to get from fighting outside the ring is people feeling, 'Oh it is getting out of hand, the referee has lost control of the match, something dangerous is about to happen'. Of course, now the

audience is used to wrestlers jumping out of the ring onto their opponents, and everyone is expecting that, but the main objective is to make people feel close to the wrestlers. They can see them centimetres away, hear the punches, moaning and groaning and panting, feel the smell of sweat and testosterone and old knee pads and trunks that haven't been washed for a month. It adds to the experience ... we are not in a closed area. I can suddenly be a part of the match, someone sitting on my lap and the other wrestlers saying 'hold him, hold him'. You are part of the match.

The power of this live moment should not be underestimated.

You can get a sense of the power in the ring, you might get a little bit pushed, or someone might sit on you. You can't compare it to physical violence in the ring, which is at higher speeds and greater force. Every wrestler knows you should be careful with the audience, you don't want to end up with someone getting hurt or scared, but we do want them to feel alive.

At one event (December 2012), two guys queued outside the venue so that they could get front row seats to their first match. Even as newcomers they expected fights spilling over from the ring. Right on cue, two pro wrestlers jumped from the ropes into the crowd; one wrestler actually sat on the guy's knee. The look on both of their faces was pure amazement. Even knowing this might happen, the power of the moment captured them completely. They explained the feeling – 'you are getting drawn into it'. And what was it that drew them? 'The audience, I would say the audience.'

REALITY ENTERTAINMENT

Similar to professional wrestling, the genre has its roots in a history of popular culture. For example, the oral ballad tradition in the eighteenth century included scurrilous crime stories from the point of view of victims and perpetrators. Victorian attractions contained variety acts, such as magic tricks, dance routines, short films and so forth. These early forms of popular culture spread through song and travelling spectaculars, and contained some of the elements we see today in reality entertainment, such as themes of crime and punishment, or variety performances. Jon Dovey in his book *Freakshows* (2000) sees connections between reality TV, with its focus on what he calls first-person media, and other kinds of populist entertainment. Whilst Dovey does not suggest reality TV is the equivalent of Victorian freakshows, he highlights the 'look at me!' and 'did you see that!' trends in the genre as it moved away from reality claims to an entertainment frame at the turn of the millennium.

The similarities between the histories of sports and reality entertainment abound. These similarities are partly to do with the development of media technologies, industry and infrastructure. Sports entertainment took off during the 1980s with the rise of cable and pay-per-view sporting events in America; reality entertainment also capitalized on a proliferation of cable channels, establishing itself as attractive content for niche audiences. As we saw in Chapter 2, the live event of reality entertainment was little used during this early period. So it is significant that when digital technologies started to make an impact on television it was reality entertainment that was the genre of choice for producers who needed hours of live and pre-recorded television that contained interactive voting, internet streaming, games and apps. Reality entertainment flourished during this key stage in the history of television. Indeed, whilst pro wrestling seems to be forever located in the 1980s, with memories of Hulk Hogan in his heyday, reality TV is the genre of the late 1990s and 2000s, and Hulk Hogan stars in a reality show (*Hogan Knows Best*, VH1 2005–7, USA).

Given the similarities between sports and reality entertainment, it is surprising how the two genres do not work well together. When you look at attempts to merge the two, there appears a division between sports promoters and producers for radio and television, and entertainment producers. Live sporting events have a look and feel that is different from reality programming. Sport borrows some of the stylistic features of reality TV but this is kept to a minimum, perhaps because the industry needs to underscore athletic values more than entertainment values in coverage of live competitions. Conversely, reality entertainment borrows extensively from sports. Professional athletes and sporting personalities work well in reality entertainment. Rugby players, cricketers and boxers often win talent shows like *Strictly Come Dancing/Dancing With the Stars* (BBC Worldwide), or they act as presenters and/or coaches of celebrities, for example figure skating champions Jane Torville and Christopher Dean in *Dancing on Ice* (ITV1, UK). Sports stadiums are used as venues for live reality events. When *Strictly Come Dancing* went to Wembley Stadium (2012), the BBC received blanket coverage in the press, reporting on the grand scale of a live event with a large crowd in a sports arena.

Sports entertainment should fill the gap between sports and reality television. It is fixed, so professionals and fans can be controlled by promoters and managers; it is a spectacle, so performance and drama are essential; and it is about characters, personalities and celebrities, so serial narratives can be created to hook consumers during events, and the spaces in between events. Sam Ford (2014) notes in 'Ten Things Corporations Can Learn from Pro Wrestling' that 'an appropriate level of spectacle is crucial', 'humour and charisma always make a connection' and 'create a serialised connection with your audience'. His top three take home points seem just as relevant to sports and entertainment industries. And yet, pro wrestling and reality television work best as separate spheres. *Celebrity Wrestling* (ITV1 2005, UK) is just one of a few flops that highlight what happens when entertainment producers make a show of pro wrestling. As cultural performances, the power of each genre lies in its specific appeal to audiences as a contradictory mix of drama and reality. Perhaps it is precisely because sports and reality entertainment are so similar that one genre cancels out the other as popular entertainment.

SPECTACULAR ENTERTAINMENT

The spectacle of reality TV has accompanied the genre since its inception. Quite a few scholarly works play on the term 'spectacle of the real', borrowing from the famous French writer Jean Baudrillard who argues that simulacra is a feature of postmodern society. He wrote scathingly of reality television as self promotion (1995). Such thinking signifies illusion, or delusion, about the representation of reality in the media. Critics of reality television use it as an example of the ultimate spectacle of the real where capitalism and consumption rule. Current writing on participatory culture and the internet draws on this thinking, using the film trilogy *The Matrix* (1999, directed by the Wachowski brothers) as a metaphor for the way commercial forces manipulate users into a delusion of free choice and participatory empowerment (see Delwiche and Henderson 2013 amongst others).

Jeffrey Sconce (2004) offers an alternative take on reality entertainment as spectacle. Although Sconce does not refer directly to Roland Barthes on the world of wrestling, the idea of a spectacle of excess runs through his writing. He calls the 'climate of panic around reality TV' in the early 2000s a 'cultural contagion' (2004: 253). After the *Big Brother* moment and the global success of competitive reality formats, there was much talk in the media and by the public about the genre as the lowest of the low. According to Sconce, 'as in most of television's previously reviled genres, reality TV requires tasteful critics to imagine an audience of cruel and gullible louts (preferably drunk) gathering to exhalt in the misfortune of others' (2004: 254). For Sconce, critics who bemoan the spectacle of reality TV miss the point: '[T]he brilliance, joy, and success of a programme like *Celebrity Boxing* stems from its very existence, regardless of what actually transpires on screen.' As he notes, 'who could resist the spectacle (or even the concept of the spectacle)' (ibid.)? Some kinds of reality TV can be a spectacle of excess, in particular competitive reality such as *American Idol*, or *I'm a Celebrity …* and *The Hunger Games*, both novels and films, satirize the spectacle of excess in competitive reality formats. These examples of reality television offer possibilities for textual play between producers, participants and audiences regarding fantasy and reality in popular culture.

Take this description of a range of reality television on offer during 2005 to British audiences:

> Let me break it down … this is crap, it is crap TV. *Big Brother, What Not to Wear*, I mean that's just like, it's a given. *Wife Swap*, crap. *The Apprentice*, crap. *The X-Factor*, beyond awful. *Plastic Surgery Live*, it's not even worthy of a comment. I have never heard of *Celebrity Love Island*, but it is all crap … *Pet Rescue*, nightmare. *Holidays from Hell,*

ridiculous. *I'm a Celebrity* ... get lost. *Faking It*, horrible ... So that's the shit pile.

(34-year-old sales consultant)

Viewers revel in the poor quality of this reviled genre.

Full Metal Jousting (USA History Channel 2012) is a good example of spectacular entertainment. Framed as historical reconstruction, the series includes violent combat. Television critic Stuart Heritage (2012) named the series his favourite of 2012 because it used 'the original extreme sport' to make television 'bloody, dangerous and thrilling'. The concept of the spectacle is to reconstruct medieval jousting as competitive reality. Men dressed in heavy armour on horseback attempt to knock each other over by jousting. Just like pro wrestling, this is a performance of unreconstructed masculinity, using violence as a key expression of feelings around power, victory, defeat and humiliation.

Mob Wives (USA, 2012) is a structured reality series set around the lives of women who are married to members of organized crime syndicates. Framed as a slice of extraordinary life, it includes over-the-top emotional dilemmas and crime and punishment crises. The scripting of *Mob Wives* means that the drama is heightened to the point of excess, so a real-life situation is shaped to maximize emotions, such as 'throw downs' between wives. This is a performance of unreconstructed femininity. The wives openly talk about their character arcs, drawn from their married lives and related to known members of organized crime, exaggerated and worked into a serial narrative. Some of the characters in *Mob Wives* have book deals, spin-off series, or own nightclubs they frequent in the series; they use Twitter to sell their persona and spread information about merchandise, or appearances during and just after a series.

June Deery (2012) calls this kind of reality TV 'staged actuality', where the 'planned and spontaneous' provide 'a powerful context for promoting specific goods and services as well as broader ideological beliefs and practices' (2012: 2). Following Baudrillard, she sees reality TV as a prime example of how mediation and consumption dominate the postmodern condition. The 'pseudo events' of reality TV are the ultimate promotion of a commercialized society. People who perform in these structured reality shows are advertising themselves as media personalities. Deery sees the very existence of reality TV as 'transforming the private from the intimate into the commercial': the genre 'illustrates how the act of mediation commercialises its own content and, by extension, real life' (2012: 174). This negative view is based on the economics of reality television within a capitalist media industry. It emphasizes economic value more than emotional, ethical or social value associated with this kind of popular entertainment.

Arlie Hochschild's (2003) work on the commercialization of intimate life is relevant. Her focus on positive expression of feelings in a commercial society works in reverse in reality television where there is a flagrant expression of feelings. This is an emotion market where expressions of violence, anger, jealousy and revenge are common currency. But these expressions are not thought to be true to life. The emotional performances are what Barthes (1972) calls the image of passion, rather than passion itself. One woman said of extreme reality TV: 'I think the reason why I love [it] so much is that it shows the extremes. Where you've got people who are just fucking extreme' (25-year-old female photographer). One 12–15-year-old girl explained why she liked the pantomime bad figure in *Big Brother*: 'Well, I think there's got to be like a bad person in TV programmes.' Another 12–15-year-old boy commented on the emotional market of reality TV: 'It's just like punching someone in the face.'

The Hollywood Reporter (2012) conducted an opinion poll of 700 American television viewers, aged 18–49, watching unscripted reality. The most hated character was The Situation from *Jersey Shore* (MTV 2009–12, USA), with 75 per cent of respondents. Next most hated was Snooki from *Jersey Shore* (65 per cent). Moreover, 30 per cent of the sample claimed the cast of the show crossed the line in taste and decency. Following closely, 64 per cent of respondents hated Kim Kardashian, and much of the cast of *Keeping Up with the Kardashians* (E! 2007–, USA): Chris Jenner (62 per cent), Kourtney Kardashian (59 per cent) and Khloe Kardashian (57 per cent). Two-thirds of the sample (68 per cent) claimed Kim Kardashian had no skills or talent. The ratings for the season finale of *Keeping Up with the Kardashians* was 3.6 million, with 2.3 million adults aged 16–49 (O'Connell 2012).

Charlie Brooker (2012) commented on hate figures in British structured reality series:

> What I am saying is the inmates of *Geordie Shore*, *The Only Way is Essex* and *Made in Chelsea* ... their job is to make absolutely everyone who tunes in hate them. Instantly hate them. Hate them so much they can't take their eyes off them ... People no longer simply aspire to be famous. They aspire to be hated. Authorised media hate figure is now a valid career ... Maybe we need these people. Maybe we are all so angry and disappointed and bewildered, we need a free bunch of people to look down on and despise ... If it wasn't for the cast of *Geordie Shore*, and countless others like them, you'd be killing your neighbours with your bare hands.

Authorised media hate figure is a good way to describe the spectacle of excess in these specific kinds of programmes. *The Only Way is Essex* (TOWIE) (ITV2 2011–) won the Bafta YouTube Audience Award in 2011. The series regularly tops the Twitter charts, filled with talk via the second screen, for example 160,000 tweets for a 2014 episode, with 35 per cent men and 65 per cent women (Secondsync 2014b). Fans are not standing in the front row booing these hate figures, but they are using the live broadcast and social media to do something similar.

Many viewers made reference to reality TV as similar to the circus, or fairgrounds, openly making a connection between the genre and a spectacle of excess. For example:

Hannah: The thing is there's getting pleasure out of seeing these people being so hideous and disgusting. (19-year-old student)

Chris: [puts on TV voice] *The X Factor* where everyone is an underdog! It is a bit like that, you know, 'everyone's an idiot'. (25-year-old illustrator)

Hannah: Right at the bottom of the pile, the real scum.

Jack: It's like a modern-day original circus. (25-year-old sound technician)

Similar to the critic Charlie Brooker (2012), these viewers caricature contestants in competitive reality formats as a 'free bunch of people to look down on and despise'.

Elias and Dunning (1986) argue that expressions of violence towards hate figures within sports, such as football, can be a rare opportunity to safely express negative feelings in a managed environment. These are feelings set against the knowledge that everyday life is characterized by anger, disappointment and bewilderment at a systemic power within a capitalist and commercial society. Sports scholars call this power play (see Boyle and Haynes 2009). The 'pleasure out of seeing these people being so hideous and disgusting' is a power play in reality entertainment that trades in negative expressions towards 'authorised media hate figures'.

Reactions to participants/contestants can be playful and problematic. Faye Woods (2012) calls British reality such as *The Only Way is Essex* a glocalization of the American form of structured reality, blurring boundaries of drama and reality, but with a sceptical, camp tone for British youth television. Series such as *Geordie Shore*, based on the American format, have a 'self aware tone, pleasure in awkwardness, and performative play' that suggests 'the innate artificiality of reality TV' (2012: 15). Woods sees a 'celebration of excess' that 'tilts towards caricature', and at the same time a 'hyper awareness of class'; this mix of messages means youth audiences engage in multiple ways, with ironic detachment and a class-based *schadenfreude* – 'thank God I am not like that'.

Beverly Skeggs and Helen Wood claim that 'reality TV has become a sustainable form of intervention into the public evaluation of people' (2012: 233). They describe a 'tournament of value', something they associate with class-based *schadenfreude*. Women watching *Wife Swap* (Channel 4 2003–, UK) trade value judgements back and forth about gender and class in Britain. Such a tournament of value can be found in Imre's research of a Hungarian reality series that features Roma participants in a much despised yet popular show. People's comments online highlight a love–hate relationship with what Imre calls racialized celebrity. He argues: '[S]hows about non white celebrities constitute a synergy between the objectionable racial quality of their protagonists and the objectionable cultural value of reality TV'

(2011: 5). Online racist comments regarding these kinds of personalities connects with other research on new racism and football fans (for example see Redhead 2014). Value judgements regarding class, gender and race, and cultural taste, complicate how people respond to participants in reality television.

Julie Donovan (2013) noted of reality television:

> It became ugly. As the producers got more desperate for that moment, it just all got vulgar ... it became clever to look for the ugly. It is like the bear pit. It is a very fine line if you are in production to producing good moments, fun moments, embarrassing moments, to actually driving vulgar people.

Viewers found certain kinds of reality TV vulgar. Some didn't like how it made them feel: 'It is just sheer entertainment, which is fine, but I don't like to be entertained that way. I mean, it's like going to bear baiting' (34-year-old male mobile phone seller). Vulgarity and spectacle was a turn off: 'I don't watch a lot of reality TV, cos I don't like to reward ugly people for being ugly. And I don't mean physically ugly, I mean ... ugly' (38-year-old female office assistant).

And for other viewers, there's a fascination with this kind of popular entertainment. One viewer reflected:

> There's almost a pleasure in being grossed out by something. It's a weird way of putting it, but there is always a sense of enjoyment, you know why do we go on fairground rides when they freak us out, but there's enjoyment at it and I think certain people get a pleasure from watching those programmes and they go 'oh, oh, that's horrible!' and they are kind of being pushed to the edge a little bit, so you know, maybe that's an appeal.
>
> (30-year-old female shop assistant)

The reality formats described in this chapter are borrowing from the cultural performance of sports entertainment, talkshows, tabloids and other kinds of popular entertainment. What marks the cultural performance of sports entertainment as different from reality entertainment is the crucial issue of liveness. There is an audience etiquette at a live pro wrestling event, where there are stage hands managing crowds, and a shared understanding of acceptable behaviour by fans and anti-fans. This management of expressions of negative emotions, performed in a pantomime manner, is not the same for reality TV audiences, in particular in their use of second screens during a live broadcast. Trolls can take a Twitter feed in negative directions, with extreme expressions regarding politics, race, class, sexuality and so forth. This is why there are different types of audience engagement with a spectacle of excess in reality formats such as *Jersey Shore* or *Geordie Shore*. Managed one way by producers, audiences, users, fans and anti-fans, there is an appeal in cheering and booing for reality performers people love and love to hate; mismanaged another way, this kind of ugly reality TV is a turn off.

FAKING IT, SMART FANS AND MARKS

Discussions of reality TV revolve around its low cultural value as popular entertainment. These discussions go right back to early forms of the genre. Take for example the furore over the first seasons of *Big Brother*. Daniel Biltereyst (2003) charted the moral panic associated with the televising of *Big Brother* in the late 1990s and early 2000s; in Portugal the national lawyers association called it the 'most vile spectacle' in the history of Portuguese television, in Germany a bishop called it 'psychic cannibalism', in France one opinion leader described it as a 'cancer of contemporary television' (2003: 93–103). More contemporary critiques of reality television audiences can be found in the satire *The Hunger Games* and the bloodthirsty crowds who jeer and cry out for violence, referencing the Roman gladiator games in ancient history.

These negative discourses of reality television tend to treat audiences as naïve, dumb or worse. Newspaper articles like 'Does Reality TV Make Us Stupid?' (Bennington 2010) signal the assumptions about audiences of this kind of popular entertainment. In an essay kit by Scope Scholastic for use in schools, the title of the essay question 'Is reality TV making you stupid?' is supported by this kind of assertion: 'Many studies say that watching too much trashy TV can cause young people to do poorly in school', or this comment: 'One of the biggest problems with reality TV is that there is nothing real about it ... but many viewers don't know that' (Scope Scholastic 2010). These assertions about dumb audiences do not take into account alternative empirical evidence from people who watch reality television.

These 12–15-year-old teenage boys reflected on the genre around the time of the first season of *Big Brother* in Britain:

Chris: That's what makes people watch it ... if something bad is happening. It's like some people watch soaps cos they see someone have a worse life than them and ...

Martin: They can feel better.

Chris: But if you've gone through it all yourself, then what's the point in watching other people do it?

Andrew: Cos they might have had a worse experience than you ...

Chris: Oh, OK.

Andrew: ... the same thing as *EastEnders* ...

John: You think 'thank god I'm not there!'

Andrew: Someone having a worse life than you, so all these things are about someone having a worse life than you ...

Kevin: Yeah, feeling a bit better than everyone else.

Chris: It's interesting, cos sometimes you're hoping that it gets better, but it never does.

This is an example of the kinds of ways young viewers engage with the inter-generic space of reality television. There is a knowing engagement with the mix of reality and drama and the sensationalizing tendencies of such a format as *Big Brother* and its claim by Endemol to be a real-life soap opera. The sense of 'thank god I'm not there!' was cited by these young viewers as one of the key attractions of the genre. Their reflection is situated in the knowledge that participants in reality formats are performing 'a worse life', knowing that this focus on emotions is 'what makes people watch it'.

What the above discussion illustrates is that it doesn't take an expert to know reality TV is not what it claims to be. Quite why audiences are thought to be ignorant of its riff on reality is one of the mysteries of the genre. It is a mystery rooted in the carny talk of smart fans and marks. A mark is someone to fool – they haven't got a clue. A smart fan needs to feel involved – chant or boo when we tell you to. This talk of the audience as marks derives from nineteenth-century carnivals and circus workers, and travelled to sports entertainment, reality entertainment and other kinds of tabloid talkshows, newspapers and magazines (see Glynn 2000 amongst others). Variations of smart fans and marks can be found in academic discussions of audiences. For example, savvy viewers are people who think they are critically aware of how the media works, but all the while they are manipulated by the industry (see Andrejevic 2009). And fan studies have examined the co-optation of fan activities and discourses into production and marketing material (see Duits, Zwaan, and Reijnders 2014).

Viewers themselves incorporate this talk of smart fans and marks into their characterization of reality contestants. For example:

Ruth: These are, a lot of people play up to the camera, they seriously want to be disrespected by Simon Cowell, because then at least there might be a chance that it could be shown on TV. So there was this couple ... and Simon Cowell said to them 'You look like Vicky Pollard from *Little Britain* [laughter], and you look like that man in drag.' And they were just 'I don't understand. What do you mean?' And then when they got off ... she said 'I would still shag him' ... they were just so desperate. These people exist, you know! (21-year-old female shop assistant)

Carl: They have no respect for themselves. (22-year-old male artist)

Ruth: Yeah, absolutely and the programme teaches them to be very degrading to themselves I think. I don't know whether or not that's how the production team manoeuvre them, but they just don't respect themselves.

Participants formerly known as the audience willingly subject themselves to what the media industry wants – they are smart fans. Jane Roscoe (2013) comments:

> Suddenly participants were media savvy, I am in control and not you. It was a reaction against producers constructing storylines and characters; they are not in charge, the participants are in charge. But when participants left the show, they would always complain about how they were portrayed and represented. The dialogue of we are in charge was used by broadcasters to promote programmes and to drive audiences to the series.

And audiences are quick to pick up on the framing of reality participants as smart fans. It is a manoeuvre on behalf of audiences to distance themselves from being seen as marks. They know that producers know that participants are being manipulated to make entertainment.

Producer intervention and backlash by the audience also occurred in talkshows such as *Jerry Springer*. Glynn notes how it is senseless to create categories of real or fake guests in tabloid talkshows as they 'depend on a certain media role playing that is demanded of everybody involved' (2000: 222, cited in Sconce 2004: 267). 'No one is surprised that the yokels on *Jerry Springer* are performing. The interest, as with much reality/tabloid TV, is in seeing how "real" people will perform their "Jerry Springer" roles' (Sconce 2004: 265). These male viewers, aged 35–50, reflected on the *Jerry Springer* effect and reality TV in 2000:

Andy: You look at *Jerry Springer* … that's a real-life programme, innit, supposed to be everyday people …
Ben: I don't know about that.
Andy: They set it all up, the fighting and that because they knew that's what people wanted to see. … People like you go out and do surveys to see what people like watching and then they organize that programme … ninety-nine out of a hundred say 'Yeah, the fighting and all that' …
Simon: It's orchestrated.
Colin: I heard they were supposed to be paying them two thousand dollars each, weren't they?

This kind of producer intervention backfires on the process of participation in reality formats, as participants/audiences became savvy about media manipulation. Shows like *Keeping Up with the Kardashians* are a case in point, where all that remains is the double manipulation of producers and participants performing for an imagined audience of marks. Hence, viewers who love to hate the Kardashians, and the rise of reality performers who aspire to be hated by the public.

PERFORMING POWER

Stephen Coleman's research on 'thinking of power in performative terms' (2010: 127) is suggestive of the particularities, contradictions and mediation of cultural performance in sports and reality entertainment. According to Coleman, power is not merely a 'substance which is used to make things happen' (2010: 129). If we consider power in performative terms then we can look at modalities of power, how it is experienced in mediated and lived realities. He explains (ibid.):

> Power tells a story of how people came to be where they are; how various sorts of interferences were introduced, received and acted upon within our lives; and how it feels to be in a world where the norms and routines of inequality are witnessed through mediated representations.

In research on participants' performances in the reality format *Big Brother*, Coleman speaks of a 'theatre of power: a space within which the witnessing audience can reflect upon the daily dilemmas of political inequality' (2010: 128).

Theatre of power is a good way to describe sports and reality entertainment. Although two different examples of popular entertainment, both illuminate what can happen when people perform power in different contexts. In sports entertainment for example, pro wrestlers routinely perform inequality in the form of class and regional dynamics, often dramatizing the unfairness of power relations through characters such as the working-class underdog from a shipbuilding city who wins against a villain from the capital.

In reality entertainment, the dilemmas of political inequality are performed differently in these contexts. Participants in structured reality, for example, may be working-class men and women but their performance of class inequality underscores feelings of difference and invites value judgements about being a single mum, or being a 'hillbilly' American family. Acting powerfully highlights the particularities and contradictions of what power looks like in different contexts and social roles.

Sports entertainment talks of audiences as marks, but this pejorative term doesn't do justice to how people are in character, just like wrestlers. At core, the power they see performed by wrestlers in violent combat in turn makes people feel powerful: 'you become strong watching them fighting. You just have a feeling that says ... I want to get in there' (male fan, December 2012). This is an example of what power looks like. Pro wrestlers, promoters and audiences offer 'a vivid representation of this dramatic contest between subjective agency and systemic power' (Coleman 2010: 145). Within the industry promoters hold power over wrestlers and their fans and anti-fans, but only to the extent that crowds as fans and anti-fans fully engage with an event. A successful event is a theatre of power where people want to witness a performance of authority, domination and unfairness by the heel, and resistance, violence and victory by the hero. The local champion, the underdog, the working-class hero, always wins; and these performances of power are set against the experiences of audiences in the dilemmas and problems of power in their everyday lives. When a live event works well, when fans and anti-fans feel strong watching wrestlers fighting, they in turn act powerfully, expressing feelings not commonly accepted in everyday social norms but considered constructive in this kind of live event. For example, when a transsexual pro wrestler spat in the face of a male anti-fan, the crowd expressed shock and excitement at this acting out of power across masculine and feminine practices (event in March 2014).

Coleman argues that reality entertainment is not an example of 'a tale of hapless and ineluctable surrender to immanent and unyielding power' (2010: 145). Similarly, sports entertainment should not be characterized as a carny trick to con consumers out of their money. Instead, what is actually happening is a 'public acknowledgement of power relations' (Coleman 2010: 145). In the case of reality entertainment, these power relations are played out between producers, participants and audiences, where the particularities of power shift according to different degrees of producer intervention, participants' performance of themselves and audience engagement. A double manipulation of producer/ participant in structured reality or talent formats means there is an audience backlash where the power dynamic shifts in favour of audiences. In the case of sports entertainment, power relations are played out in a combination of drama, ritual and sport, where promoters and wrestlers invite audiences to be a driving force in a high-energy, adrenalin-fuelled event. People's passionate expressions at pro wrestling live events or people's engagement with reality TV are not an illusion of participation, nor a suspension of disbelief, but cultural performances in a theatre of power. As this pro wrestler explained: 'It is me with the volume turned up to eleven' (Ahtola 2013).

CONCLUSION

Sports and reality entertainment are commonly described as trash culture. To counteract such a claim, some critics have pointed out how professional wrestlers train hard, or that members of the public are represented within a range of reality programming. But this kind of entertainment is trash culture, loud and proud. Roland Barthes (1957) wrote that wrestling is a spectacle of excess. Passions are exaggerated and characters display big physical and emotional performances concerning light and dark, fair play and foul play. We can say something similar about reality entertainment, in particular, structured reality and mega formats. Subtlety and ambiguity are not the main attraction of pro wrestling or formatted reality today, instead power play is the name of the game.

Sports and reality entertainment are dogged by accusations of fakery. Here, the explicitly negative critique that professional wrestling is fixed, or reality television is scripted, is probably the most common means of denigrating both examples of popular culture. Certainly, professional wrestling up until the 1980s promoted itself as live sports to its consumers, attempting to keep the choreography of the craft as industry knowledge. After some scandals during this decade regarding fixed matches, pro wrestling re-launched itself as entertainment where the dramatic character and spectacle of the sport was more openly acknowledged by the industry and its fans. Similarly, reality television started out in the 1980s and 1990s making some claims to authenticity, with producers and broadcasters promoting series with public service or documentary credentials. After some scandals in the 1990s regarding producer intervention, the success of competitive reality allowed the industry to promote the genre as entertainment that included some elements of casting, scripting and characterization. Today, pro wrestling and reality TV crowds and audiences know that fights are fixed and formats are staged events. People are attracted to these forms of entertainment in part because they are high drama. But there is also an emotional truth within the spectacle of excess. This emotional truth can be about how a wrestler plays a character but can still take a beating, or how a participant in a reality format is performing but can still move viewers in some way. By acknowledging what is staged and dramatic, sports and reality entertainment engages audiences in playful arenas that sit between fact and fiction.

Coupled with claims of fakery, wrestling fans are usually described as smart fans and marks. A smart fan is someone who works for professional wrestlers and promoters without realizing they are producing free labour. A mark comes from carnival workers who saw customers as easy marks for making money. These negative descriptions of consumers as smart fans or marks are very similar to descriptions of reality TV viewers. Audiences are often framed as fools who believe in the truth claims of reality TV and pay good money to do so, or savvy viewers exploited by the industry to produce free labour through the illusion of interaction and participation. It is certainly the case that sports and reality entertainment consumers and audiences are subject to structural forces within these industries. When fans buy a ticket for a match or viewers vote for their favourite contestants, they are part of an emotional economics. But these people are also part of shaping an emotional narrative through their individual and collective practices. In particular, the passionate engagement of fans and anti-fans points to the knowing activity of audiences. Terms like smart fans or marks fail to take into account how audiences are part of a collective self-conscious engagement with these examples of trash culture.

Both types of entertainment could be described as cultural performances in a theatre of power, following Stephen Coleman's (2010) description of performances of power in reality television. In the live theatre of power that is pro wrestling, there is the spontaneous power of a moment-to-moment experience that grabs and takes a hold of the crowd, and there is the scripting of passions, and excessive performances within and outside of the ring. In the live broadcasts and second screen activities of reality entertainment, a theatre of power is experienced in different ways depending on the live event of a format, social viewing and social media commentary. Audiences and social media users can drop in and out of a television series so this lessens the moment-by-moment experience of a live event, but the scripting and spontaneity of excessive emotional performances is a key feature of structured reality or competitive reality formats. The liveness of pro wrestling allows for management of the powerful performances between pro wrestlers and their fans and anti-fans. The live broadcast and pre-recorded status of reality television means performances of power can be mis-managed by producers, participants and audiences, so there are mixed feelings of power play, and misuse of power in this kind of entertainment. Expressions of hatred can crossover from pantomime performance into social media trolls and hate texts. At its most playful, sports and reality entertainment are examples of acting powerfully. Set against a backdrop where we are expected to exercise emotional control, to solve problems ourselves, where we often feel powerless in the face of state institutions, this is an attractive entertainment experience.

6

CONCLUSION
REALITY BITES

TV has become such an intricate part of who we are.

(40-year-old male retail worker)

Reality television is popular entertainment. And yet a common way to start a conversation about it is 'I wouldn't want anyone to know this but ... '. It is a guilty genre because people often watch it in secret. Say 'reality TV' and first impressions are often negative. Critics have predicted its negative impact on modern culture; protesters have railed against its existence; participants have sued producers for exploitation; and viewers have called it car crash TV. In the novel *Dexter is Delicious* by Jeff Lindsay (2010: 279), the character of a teenage girl comments on her secret desire to be eaten by cannibals. She asks Dexter, a serial killer who stalks other killers: 'Don't you have some kind of secret that, you know ... you can't help it, but it makes you kind of ashamed?' 'Sure' Dexter replies, 'I watched a whole season of *American Idol*.'

It is precisely because reality television is popular entertainment that it is often perceived as a guilty pleasure. Entertainment formats like *Idol* utilize multi-media, taking the television pro-gramme and widening its points of consumption to include live events, micro payments, second screens, national tours, toys and merchandise, and so forth. Everywhere people turn, there is the brand, the merchandise, the chance to make money through advertising, ticket sales, downloads and apps. Similar to the sporting industry, reality television has been accused of over-commercializing the genre to the point of saturation. Such a cri-ticism overstates the brand value of reality television. According to Gary Carter, 'fiction television brands (like *Dr Who*) are far more successfully exploited in the "real world" than reality series are, despite claims' (2014). But this attitude towards the new economy of reality television that trades on brand, personality, emotion and ethics goes some way to explaining the over-whelming negative critique of the genre. One of the challenges to understanding reality television is to both acknowledge this negative critique of the market of 'reality' in a commercial society and also see the multiple ways audiences and publics, consumers and users, engage with 'reality' relations.

The argument of this book is that audience engagement with different types of reality television tells us something about why people love and love to hate this form of popular entertainment. This concluding chapter examines the key themes of the book. These themes include the phenomenon of reality TV as a new kind of inter-generic space; the escalation of reality entertainment for-mats and producer intervention; audiences, fans and anti-fans for reality TV; the spectacle of reality and sports entertainment; and the ways real people and celebrities perform themselves in cross-media content. Reality TV has been a major entertainment genre of the past 15 years. But it is a fading phenomenon at this juncture in time. Jane Roscoe (2013), from SBS, notes: 'Where are the shows that still make us say "oh that is great?" Reality TV has led the way, but dramas are the formats of the now.' What the future holds is an open question for this form of popular enter-tainment. Yet, reality TV is a cannibal, feeding off the success of other genres, like sports or soap opera, and trends such as second screens and emotional economics. In this sense it is a resilient cultural form that feeds off itself and moves on (Sassoon 2006).

The chapter ends with the return to authenticity within reality television. For the past 15 years reality TV has moved away from the small moments in everyday life to the big moments of tears and tantrums. It has gone so far down the scripted and structured route that there is a hunger once again for the authentic. How authenticity is produced within television creates an interesting dynamic concerning realist aesthetics, for example under-producing a reality series, showing back-stage moments, or rough camera work. And there is a dynamic concerning a play off between performance and authenticity. This reconnection with the ordinary suggests a different kind of 'reality' relations at work in the next formation of reality entertainment.

MULTIPLE REALITIES

Much debate about reality television is concerned with definitions. Is reality TV a genre that can be defined as an object of study? Is it a phenomenon that can be understood in popular culture? Is it an industry trend that introduces a new economics of reality television? Reality TV is all of these things. It is a porous genre in the sense that the characteristics of reality television blur boundaries between fact and entertainment. It is a phenomenon in the sense that reality television has broad generic occurrence, popping up in different types of popular entertainment, and it has phenomenal moments within individual series or programmes that grab audience and user attention. It is an example of a new type of emotional or experience economy within the television, internet and marketing industry that trades not only on the use value of a product but also the market of emotions in a commericalized society (Hochschild 2003). John Corner (2014) notes, 'reality TV is a really a new kind of inter-generic space.' This comment highlights how reality television resists containment. Producers, participants and audiences draw on different genres, and social and cultural trends, to create a new kind of inter-generic space for cross-media content.

According to Gary Carter (2013), 'reality television is becoming invisible: it is hard to identify what it is, precisely, and yet its implications are seen everywhere, even in the news. It has become an effect, more than a genre'. To say there is a reality television effect is similar to the idea of a porous genre, something often associated with hybrid genres like drama documentary (see Paget 1998). The porous, or leaky, genre of drama documentary bleeds into dramas that claim a fictional story is based on true events; it bleeds into factual genres that use reconstructions and stylized dramatizations to tell a true story. Drama documentary is a hybrid of other genres, and as it becomes established in its own right as a form of production with codes, conventions, ethics and practices, it starts to impact on other cultural forms. Paget (1987) points out how contemporary verbatim theatre borrows from drama documentary traditions; this kind of theatre uses transcripts of trial testimony, or historical records, to dramatize a true event. For example, *London Road* (National Theatre 2011) is a theatrical musical, written by Alecky Blythe, based on interviews of people who lived next door to a serial killer.

As an inter-generic space, reality television codes and conventions, ethics and practices, resist containment. In earlier research on factuality (Hill 2007), I called reality TV a feral genre, using the metaphor to suggest how the genre was not self-contained, stable or knowable, but de-territorial and wildly opportunistic. What happens when a feral genre is left unchecked? During the 1990s, the genre was a blend of factual, fictional and light entertainment, but it was still a genre you could pin down and locate within the television industry. After competitive reality, the genre became a worldwide phenomenon. There is such a broad landscape of reality television that it defies definition.

Jonathan Bignell wrote in *Big Brother: Reality TV in the Twenty-first Century* (2005: 172) that 'the whole purpose of this book is to question what is at the centre of reality TV, and to question what we mean by the term at all'. He explains:

> The question of how to evaluate reality TV depends first on identifying what it is. This initial identification, in relation to media other than television, and in relation to genres and forms within television culture is problematic. The problem is partly because of reality TV's assimilation of elements of various fictional and factual television forms, partly a matter of its audience address, partly a matter of its

institutional position in the output of broadcasters and partly a matter of the blurring of boundaries between intratextual and extratextual elements such as related products of media practices like Internet interactivity.

(2005: 176–77)

Bignell argues that 'reality TV is not a genre, but an attitude to the functions of television, its audiences and its subjects' (2005: 172).

To say reality television is not a genre but an attitude is to question the core of reality TV. One viewer in the mid-2000s described it as empty:

It's an empty vessel, you know you can pour something that's completely morally appalling into it, or you can pour something that's really constructive … you can do anything you like with it.

(60-year-old male design consultant)

In this sense, reality television is hard to define because people can create their own version of reality.

For example, is *Benefits Street* (Channel 4 2014, UK) 'something that's really constructive' or 'something that's completely morally appalling'? The Factual Creative Director of Love Productions said 'it is really important to show parts of Britain that aren't normally on TV' (Aitkenhead 2014). A news article on the series came with the headline 'Decoding *Benefits Street*: How Britain was Divided by a Television Show' (Price 2014); those of the political left saw the series as demonizing the poor; and those on the right saw it as a wake-up call for hard-working families screwed by benefits scum (ibid.). Despite, or perhaps because of, its widespread controversy, the series attracted audiences of five million, a record high for the channel that received similar ratings for its coverage of the Paralympics in London 2012. In terms of second screen activity, one episode attracted 55,993 tweets, 57 per cent male and 43 per cent female, with a popular hashtag of parasite street, and comments such as 'poverty my arse' (Secondsync 2014a). It received 1,800 complaints to the Office of Communications. People participating in the series attracted negative and positive attention from the media, politicians and the public. Deirdre Kelly, AKA White Dee, was called by a Tory MP 'too common for the House of Commons', professional trolls tweeted that her children should be taken into care; she appeared on live television debates, and received offers to participate in competitive reality shows like *I'm a Celebrity ... Get Me Out of Here!* (ITV1, UK) (Aitkenhead 2014). White Dee now has an agent and is described in the press as a 'professional reality TV contestant'. She explained: '[T]he show did us bad – but no one would give two hoots about what I had to say before. If we can make good out of it, then brilliant' (Aitkenhead 2014). Without a fixed and knowable centre, reality TV becomes what people want it to be.

The implications of reality television as a new kind of inter-generic space are everywhere. A reality style can be detected in drama, such as reality contestants hired as actors in soap operas. *The Office* (BBC 2001–3, UK; NBC 2005–13, USA) is a mock docusoap, with comedic actors performing as if they are ordinary people participating in an observational reality programme. A reality style features in radio and journalism, such as radio phone-ins with reality contestants, or tabloid news about winners and losers of reality formats. It occurs in print publishing, like autobiographies of reality TV celebrities. *The Hunger Games* by Suzanne Collins is a novel and film series set in a dystopian world, satirizing competitive reality formats.

Reality television prefigured performance of the self online, in the form of surveillance and webcams, or digital storytelling of everyday people. The Susan Boyle effect is a trope of talent show audition filmed in bite-sized form for YouTube. The music industry is intertwined with talent formats, launching the latest reality TV winner with a debut album, tour and personal appearances. Reality TV influences theatre, such as musical stars discovered in reality talent contests. Dance shows have led to public interest in ballroom dance classes, or live tours of professional and celebrity dance routines. It impacts on sports, for example talent show winners singing at the Super Bowl. Reality themes influence the arts, such as exhibitions about the politics of surveillance and voyeurism. It influences fashion in the form of models from talent formats, or reality celebrity perfumes and clothing brands. Reality series such as *The Bachelor* inspire tourism and leisure experiences. Reality television even connects with religion, for example reality stars like the Kardashian family purchasing churches with exclusive membership of a personalized religion, or contestants on *American Idol* promoting their religious beliefs through choice of songs.

Reality television makes visible its own mediation process. Douglas Wood (2013), Head of Audience Research at Shine Group, comments:

> Now viewers are watching something as real when they know it is artificial. That is the *Big Brother* generation who now accept the rules of TV. 'Fair enough, you have told us what is happening here. We know it is constructed, we know the rules. We can now watch and enjoy the show.' It fascinates me, this blend of fact and fiction. It is a real paradox that as a viewer you are told up front that this is artificial and constructed, but you still buy into it as a real life.

Here then, soft-scripted reality series such as *The Only Way is Essex* invite a *Big Brother* generation into the mediated space of the genre.

Pål Hollender (2014), Executive Producer at Shine Nordic, reflects on the mediation process:

> In the television world I am worried about reality shows. I think it is horrific that we go more and more towards scripted reality. That is not even fake; it is counterproductive. It's like the devil in the perception of reality. You tell other people that normal people experience life in a certain way when it has no relation whatsoever to what these people actually experience in their life. I have strong feelings about how the producer should treat reality, just going there and letting the script write itself, when you actually see what is happening.

The devil in reality television is a counterproductive tendency to intervene in people's experiences of social life. The scripted reality of *Here Comes Honey Boo Boo* (TLC 2012–, USA) has little relation to life in America. As Hollender notes, 'there's nothing there but one liners' (2014).

These viewers commented on a reality format:

Laura: What's *The X Factor*? (37-year-old female art seller)
Mark: What is *The X Factor*? [repeats shocked]. *The X Factor* is ... (34-year-old male mobile phone consultant)
Laura: Is it a show where they sing?
Mark: They sing or they do stunts too, so it's like *Pop Idol*.
Sally: That's where the judges, you know, really take the mickey. (32-year-old female personal assistant)

This kind of talent show is taking the mickey out of itself. 'The more horrible they sing on *The X-Factor* you think "god, yeah". There are some things you just can't take your eyes off, like car crash TV' (21-year-old female shop assistant). For the 2013 finale of *The X Factor* in the UK, the Saturday show featured former bad acts like Wagner, who received the peak tweets for that episode (Secondsync 2013; 511,184 tweets in total for those memorable acts). Compare this to the announcement of the winner (21,000 tweets).

Comedian Harry Hill described how reality TV has come to satirize itself. He stopped making the television satire *TV Burp* (ITV1 2001–10, UK) partly because of scripted reality: 'It was getting tougher to write because everything started having an ironic voiceover. The killer was *The Only Way is Essex*, we couldn't do anything with that. Or we felt like people were actually trying to get on *TV Burp*' (Petridis 2014). The idea behind the musical *I Can't Sing!* was to satirize this hunger to be on television at any cost. A musical satire of reality TV was a risky venture, after the failure of *Viva Forever!* the Spice Girls musical that spoofed talent shows. Less than two months after opening night at the London Palladium, the show closed, despite decent reviews of its 'eye-smartingly bad taste' (Press Association 2014). A theatre critic (Billington 2014) explained:

> A vast amount of time, talent, energy and money (£6 million of it) is expended on telling us that TV talent shows are self-aggrandising charades beset by internal politics and dominated by vanity. I suspect many of us had worked this out already.

After the closure of *I Can't Sing!*, a commentator said: 'It always had the smell of death about it' (Press Association 2014).

This sense of 'there's no such thing as reality' relies on a knowingness between producers, participants and audiences. In a novel by John le Carré, a secret spy reflects on the process of deception: '[N]o two bluffs are the same, but one component is necessary to all of them, and that is a complicity between the deceiver and the deceived, the mystical interlocking of opposing needs' (le Carré 1993: 556). When it fails, reality TV is the bluff that no one is deceived by, falling short of the necessary components to pull off a grand deception. But when it works, there is a complicity between producers, participants and audiences about 'reality' relations in television and in everyday life.

AUDIENCES, FANS AND ANTI-FANS

In the book *Audiences: A Sociological Theory of Performance and Imagination*, Abercrombie and Longhurst (1998) identify previous paradigms of mass or diffused audiences, and present a paradigm of spectacle/performance as the dominant framework for understanding audience processes. A spectacle/performance paradigm is about a 'circuit of spectacle and narcissism', 'the way in which spectacle leads to the aestheticisation of everyday life, and the constitution of the narcissistic society of modernity' (1998: 2). For Abercrombie and Longhurst audiences are part of different communities, using their imagination, skills, resources and enthusiasms to perform being an audience or fan. A spectacle/performance paradigm means audiences perform their identities, in a circuit of spectacle and narcissism that is part of the mediascape (1998: 37).

The idea of spectacle is helpful for understanding the kinds of audiences that are drawn to certain types of reality television, such as competitive reality or reality soaps. Whilst Abercrombie and Longhurst use narcissism to work through the psychological processes in the spectacle of being an audience, we can extend the notion of identity and performance to social interaction as well. A circuit of spectacle and narcissism implies audiences are caught in a loop of performing different roles as viewers, users, consumers, audiences and publics in a late-modern, self-reflexive society

(1998: 37). Joshua Meyrowitz (1985) used another idea of performance that was inspired in part by Erving Goffman's concept of performance of the self (1959). This social interaction approach to audiences extends the idea of spectacle and performance beyond narcissism and psychological interpretations to include the situated nature of being an audience. Meyrowitz describes the social situation of performer–audience relations: we are 'all performing roles in new theatres that demand new styles of drama' (1985: 309). As we shall see, the play off between spectacle and performance of the self is central to understanding reality television audiences.

What it is like to be an audience for reality television? We can map different viewing cultures for different kinds of reality television, from general audiences, to fans, guilty viewers and binge viewers, and reality refusniks. Briefly, there are viewers who watch a series occasionally or regularly; these are by far the most common form of audiences for reality programming as diverse as talent shows, reality soaps and lifestyle. For executive producers, these audiences are made visible as consumers and users, via ratings data for live and catch-up audiences, and social media analytics (see Napoli 2010). There are fans who engage with a series and make time to follow it, and who may share their favourite series with family and friends, or write a blog. For industry audience research, there are degrees of fandom; fans are people who really engage and commit to a series, recommending it to others, sharing and commenting on social media, and superfans are those that perhaps other fans follow as elite bloggers, or they might be people who eventually become participants themselves, a superfan now known as a reality contestant.

The low cultural value attributed to reality television can sometimes bring about guilty engagement. A guilty viewer talks about certain types of reality shows, such as competitive reality or particular talent formats, as a bad addiction, one they should try to break. Talent shows usually run for months: there are daily updates and live events scheduled as a big appointment to view, with voting, second screen activity, mobile apps, and former contestants promoting themselves in talkshows, newspapers and gossip magazines. Audiences of a format like *Big Brother*, or

American Idol, describe binging on the show during these programmes, live events and social media, and then feeling guilty
about the time and emotional energy they have devoted to such a
show. The low cultural value of some competitive reality formats
frames these viewers' guilty consumption. They vow not to
watch, and then find themselves once again caught in the
momentum of the next episode, live event and Twitter trend.
One fan described her engagement as 'full-on *Big Brother*' (12–15-
year-old female). Another fan explained: 'I don't know, I thought
it was actually rubbish that programme but I was so hooked
I had to keep watching it! You just had to see what was going on
the following day … there was no really story to it, I just … got
hooked into it' (29-year-old female office worker).

There is another kind of audience engagement that is often
described in everyday discussion as binge viewing. Binge fans
engage in another way with reality television. This kind of fan is
binging on something they really like, saving up time to spend
watching their favourite show. Such a fan may still characterize
their engagement as an addiction, but this is a guilt-free addiction. Arlie Hochschild talks about 'a time bind' in which people
are caught in the stresses of work and life in a commercialized
society (2003). Binge fans save time in their busy everyday lives
to enjoy a special moment of engagement with a favourite form of
media content. If there can be such a thing as positive binging,
then these fans shore up the scarce resource of time to cram hours
of a series into a personalized time zone. This shoring up of time
for binge fandom highlights an attachment to cultural artefacts,
something noted within fan studies and psychological modes of
engagement (see Sandvoss 2005 and Hills 2002, amongst others).
Some reality formats attract this kind of strong engagement from
fans. Shiny floor shows like *Strictly Come Dancing/Dancing with the
Stars* (BBC Worldwide) have binge fans who shore up their show
to watch and interact with at special times created just for this
experience. One binge fan watched *Strictly* on a Saturday evening,
and then re-watched her favourite moments on a Sunday after-
noon whilst doing the ironing, always at the same time after the
ritual of Sunday lunch. But we see binge fans of this kind much
more often with drama. *Game of Thrones* (HBO 2011–) is a drama

trend that sports binge fans like a badge of honour. Latecomers to *Breaking Bad* (AMC 2008–13) played catch-up on previous seasons to reach the finale, thus creating a new trend where the final season of a drama garners an increase in ratings. Netflix even promotes special drama series like *House of Cards* (2013–) to a target audience of binge fans, releasing the second season all in one go on Valentine's Day 2014.

There are also anti-fans who actively dislike a series, keep up to date with news and social media about it, and make time to express their negative views (see Gray 2003). Anti-fans include reality refusniks (Hill 2007). These are people who refuse to watch reality television as a point of honour. Here is one male viewer, retired, voicing his anti-reality TV position: 'Thousands of so-called reality programmes. These are devastating television programmes to the detriment of viewing. It is a descent into the pit.' Reality refusniks are very vocal, writing books, giving high-profile lectures at industry events, going on talkshows and televised debates, making official complaints, establishing campaigns against reality television. The recent example of *Benefits Street* highlights the activity, energy and general acceptance of anti-reality TV discourses, especially when they combine with anti-benefits discourses.

When audiences adopt anti-reality TV discourses, they often describe it as popular entertainment. Joke Hermes (1995) discussed women's magazines as easy to put down, something readers excused as a guilty habit. In this discussion with a family in 2001, a daughter and mother excuse watching *Popstars* (ITV1 2001, UK), a precursor to the talent formats that we see now:

Sandra: It's like you pick up glossy magazines in the shops, well the girls do, and flip through all the magazines like *Now* and all things like that … see what they're wearing …

Victoria: Yeah, I think it is the relaxation thing as well. It doesn't get too deep. Like I said, it's quite superficial.

Victoria's son strongly denied watching *Popstars*, and was proud to say it: 'I didn't like *Popstars* at all … No, I didn't watch a single one.' The gender divide with talent shows, just like glossy magazines, makes it easy to dismiss as mindless entertainment aimed at women. As Sandra said: 'it's more of a girl thing, you know.'

Reality television audiences switch between different types of viewers, fans and anti-fans, for different kinds of reality television. So much depends on content, mood and context. For example, viewers for reality talent formats such as *American Idol* are part of a national live event, and some will be fans who regularly vote and show up to the live shows. These same audiences and fans will also be aware there are anti-fans who actively dislike *Idol* and what it represents to them in terms of commercial television or the music industry. In another example, viewers for a reality series like *The Hotel* (BBC 2013) are audiences for broadcast television, or catch-up viewers online, and the series is something to talk about during the week with friends and family. These same viewers may well associate docusoaps like this one with mock series such as *The Office* and find a wry humour in the mundanity of the day-to-day running of the hotel.

Discourses of audiences in industry and academic contexts try to label people as one thing or another. But audiences are often performing several roles at the same time for very different kinds of reality television. Take this young female viewer (aged 12–15 years old) of the British *Big Brother* in 2000:

> I didn't like it at first, ... I was away for a month and I came back and everyone was talking about it. I was like 'What on earth is it?' I didn't know what the big thing was. I put it on and I was like 'This is a joke, this is pathetic!' And then my brother kept having it on, I kept watching and I got so into it! I was addicted! I was mad, I was like 'I love it, I love it, I love it!' So I ended up absolutely loving it and then it stopped and I was crying! I was crying at the end! [laughs] I got so into it I started crying!

Such an example shows audiences switch back and forth between positive and negative modes of engagement. Indeed, this young viewer went from refusnik ('this is pathetic!') to engaged viewer ('I got so into it!') to fan ('I love it, I love it I love it!'). Such a viewer can just as easily switch to negative engagement depending on their reactions to other series.

Mark Lawson commented on the market for anti-reality TV content, such as satirical novels and film series like *The Hunger Games*. He notes that 'teenagers who are the main target audience for Collins' savage satire of Cowellesque television are also the primary consumers of talent and reality shows in their original form' (Lawson 2014). Teenagers are also the main targets as contestants in competitive reality. For reality television, there is not one type of audience, but rather people switch between different modes of engagement, performing the roles of viewers, consumers, fans, anti-fans, critics and participants.

SPORTS AND REALITY ENTERTAINMENT

Professional wrestling provides an illustration of an entertainment spectacle that is useful for thinking about reality television. Sports entertainment of the kind we might see in American World Wrestling Entertainment or Mexican *lucha libre* is highly physical, emotional and performative. Heather Levi (2008) describes the acrobatic wrestling style of Mexican *lucha libre* as a cultural performance, following the work of Richard Schechner (1977) and Victor Turner (1986). Levi argues that the contradictions of drama and sport make the spontaneous and ritualized acts of pro wrestlers and crowds powerful cultural performances relating to areas of gender, nationality and politics. This combination of performance, spectacle and emotion in professional wrestling can help us to understand the higher emotional states in reality entertainment. In particular, we can draw on professional wrestling to explore what makes reality television a cultural co-performance by producers, participants and audiences.

Roland Barthes (1972) wrote about the world of wrestling as a spectacle of excess, a popular drama of good and evil. This was at a point in the history of professional wrestling in the post-war period where pre-determined endings were supposed to be an insider secret. Barthes acknowledged the drama and performance in professional wrestling; he described people as captured by the moment, experiencing an image of passion rather than passion

Figure 6.1 Mime and clown (Dan Ahtola and Eddie Vega). Photograph: Michael Rübsamen.

itself. Once American professional wrestling re-invented itself as sports entertainment in the 1980s, the scripting and ritual elements of live matches became even more spectacular, as characters and serialized narrative arcs accompanied celebrity wrestlers who performed as heroes and heels in violent contests.

The contradictions of sports entertainment generate speculation about professional practices and crowd reactions to a spectacle of excess. Are wrestlers faking it? Do audiences believe what they see? Research on pro wrestlers shows that although they perform in pre-determined matches, the punches, bruises and pain they experience are real (Tyson Smith 2008). Beekman (2006) notes how pro wrestlers have poor life expectancy, especially those that perform in American WWE. Within the sports entertainment industry, insider language labels crowds as 'smart fans' or 'marks', both terms derogative of people as easy marks to make money from. The language is drawn from Victorian carnival talk and seems out of touch considering people's engagement with contemporary sports entertainment. Pro wrestler Dan Ahtola (2013) comments: 'The reactions and the emotions from the audience are not fake, made up, not trained before. It is a spontaneous, genuine reaction to something they know is a show. What is happening?'

What is happening is that pro wrestlers work together as emotional co-labour, using physical and emotional performances to generate audience excitement. One wrestler described this as: 'It's me with the volume turned up to eleven' (Ahtola 2013). In turn the crowd also work together to feed this excitement back to pro wrestlers. There are different types of engagement with these live collective performances at pro wrestling events. The people in the first few rows are the most passionately engaged; they perform as fans and anti-fans, in character with the volume turned up to 11. If you sit in the front rows you are hoping for action. People in the next set of seats have mixed modes of engagement, physically reacting to the match and socializing with friends at the venue. Those at the back, or in the higher tier seating, are popping in and out of these collective performances, sometimes reacting as one with the crowd and other times performing as fans and anti-fans. Just because both wrestlers and their audience are performing passion this does not mean there is no passion itself. There are genuine reactions that come from acting with emotional excess.

Reality entertainment follows a similar trajectory to sports entertainment. There was a period in the development of the genre in the 1990s where news and documentary sensibilities were mixed within an entertainment frame – hence the genre was commonly called factual entertainment or infotainment. There were series that flirted with fakery in the 1990s but the whole genre was not perceived as entirely made up. Somewhere in the 2000s the staging of reality became more obvious. These viewers reflected on this process during the mid-2000s:

Roger: It's just so fake. (35-year-old male train track operator)
Mark: But the thing is, it used to be, I think with the reality TV programme, it actually started out as something ... on the BBC, but then it sort of became a mass-market TV format ... (34-year-old male mobile phone consultant)
Laura: It is like that MTV show that was on years ago, *The Real World*, I thought that was a bit better. (37-year-old female art seller)
Mark: But that was completely scripted.
Martin: Yeah, it was. (34-year-old male sales consultant)
Laura: Maybe that's why it was better.

Here then, reality TV is associated with popular entertainment that is considered scripted and fake.

There is also speculation about participants and audiences of reality entertainment. Do participants fake it? Do audiences believe what they see? Contestants in competitive reality or talent formats claim they wish to share their personal experience with the public. This viewer commented:

I don't get what makes reality TV? Reality TV is a scripted environment filled with D-list people who are desperate enough to try and become C-list ... people. It's just really kind of ... it's sad, it's people on display, it's people displaying in a scripted environment their worst characteristics, because that's all the reason why people watch it, to find out the dirt and ... it's a forced environment.

(60-year-old male design consultant)

Participants in these kinds of reality television are rarely perceived as ordinary people – they are a new breed of wannabe celebrities.

Terms such as 'savvy viewers' describe reality television audiences who labour under the misconception that they know what is going on when all the time these consumers are easy marks for the media industry. Such a way of seeing audiences of reality television is similar to that of the terms smart fans and marks within professional wrestling. But audiences do know what is happening. One viewer summed up reality TV as 'there's no such thing as absolute truth. But with this, let's say it right at the beginning' (25-year-old female photographer). Another viewer described the format of *Faking It* (RDF Media) as 'you fake it, and then you try to go for it' (25-year-old female waitress). We could say something similar is happening when audiences knowingly riff on reality.

To play on the terms smart fans and marks, audiences can switch roles when watching, interacting and participating in reality entertainment. Some types of reality television, like *Keeping Up with the Kardashians*, make viewers feel more like marks. There is explicit reference to branding and the commercialization of intimate life (Hochshchild 2003). You can feel duped when watching a show like this. It is no wonder the Kardashians top charts for personalities people love to hate; reality soaps often feature what Charlie Brooker calls authorized media hate figures (2012). Other types of reality television, such as talent show *Strictly Come Dancing*, make viewers feel more like smart fans, invited to help create the outcome of an event through watching, interacting and voting. You can feel pulled into a show like this. The invitation to audiences is as participants who are the stars of the show. These feelings of being duped, or pulled into a show, can alternate in the same media experience. So you can find yourself pulled into a moment of family drama in *Here Comes Honey Boo Boo*, despite an overall sense of being a mark for producers and participants of this reality soap. Or you can find yourself pulling back from a moment of producer intervention in *Strictly Come Dancing*, despite an overall sense of being a smart fan for this shiny floor show.

Although the sports entertainment industry sees all audiences as marks, any good promoter and professional wrestler knows that without smart fans a match would be a great disappointment. Promoters and wrestlers feed off the energy of smart fans, working with them all the time during pre-match, live-at-an-event and post-match experiences. Any audience member for pro wrestling knows this, indeed expects to perform as smart fans. There is something similar at work in the reality entertainment industry. The marketing for this kind of popular entertainment sees audiences mainly as consumers. But any good producer, participant or professional performer knows that without smart fans a series is likely to flop. Finding ways to keep in step with contemporary audiences and users as they switch between the roles of smart fans and marks is a challenge for reality television. Key is to cultivate emotional connections, to acknowledge the contradictions within the cultural performance of reality television.

For example, two newcomers to professional wrestling chatted on the train home about their experience that night at a wrestling event (Malmo, December 2013). These undergraduate students in their early twenties were still on a high from the live experience. One of them was hooked, a fresh fan, so excited they wanted to start training as a wrestler. His friend started to downplay their experience, commenting on how fake pro wrestling was: 'It's fun, but nothing special.' The fresh fan pulled out his mobile phone. 'So who is this, then?' showing footage of his friend screaming at the top of his voice, cheering and booing for heroes and heels. Here, we see a transition between different modes of engagement, performing being an audience, fan and anti-fan, switching roles in the moment-to-moment experience.

PERFORMING THE SELF

A central argument in this book is that the concept of the performance of the self is a defining feature of reality television. The concept originates in sociologist Erving Goffman's book *The*

Presentation of Self in Everyday Life (1959). Joshua Meyrowitz reflected on reading Goffman as a college student in 1960s America:

> Goffman describes social life as a kind of multi-stage drama in which we perform different roles in different arenas, depending on the nature of the situation, our particular role in it, and the makeup of the audience ... Goffman made me aware of perceptions and actions that are normally intuitive and unconscious.
>
> (1985: 2)

Meyrowitz took Goffman's original concept and updated it in his study of media and society, *No Sense of Place* (1985). He opened up the concept to account for front, middle-region and back-stage peformances of the self, arguing that the dynamism of Goffman's social drama needed to be extended to broader social, political and technological changes. He argued that television and a media matrix displaced communities and families. Meyrowitz saw a placeless culture in the America of the Reagan years, detecting a 'meism' (1985: 318) in the politics and society of the time.

Goffman's premise of social life as a multi-stage drama needs to be staged differently for contemporary media. Yet, the characteristics he identified with performing the self at work or at home transfer to today's media rather well. For example, his idea of a front and back stage self highlights how people switch between public and private personas. Or, the notion that people draw on props or resources to enhance performances illuminates the value of culture, objects and social relations in the scripting of a performance in different stage settings. Goffman's attention to the role of the audience also suggests that we perform with an audience in mind, and adjust our performances depending on their expectations or reactions. Goffman did not foresee social life integrated with digital media technologies, but the performance of selves can be seen in various forms of the internet. Some scholars argue we live a media life (Deuze 2012), which might imply all social life is a multi-media drama. Certainly *The Truman Show* (1998, director Peter Weir) comes to mind as the ultimate, dystopian end to the performance of the self in a media matrix (see Delwiche and Henderson 2013).

Gary Carter (2013) comments that 'from a television point of view what is interesting is the way technology allowed certain things to happen, the river of material rather than the smallest possible stream'. What is so significant about reality television is that it came at just the right moment in the development of digital technology where a river of material could flow across multi-media. Competitive formats such as *Big Brother*, *Survivor* and *The X Factor* made social life a multi-stage drama on a mega scale. At first, the performance of the self was staged within the little moments of everyday social interaction. Participants in early seasons of *Big Brother* learned how to perform themselves and compete in a gameshow. Audiences watched ordinary people perform on the television and internet, they interacted through voting and reflected on the social roles we play in everyday life, the characters we try out and discard, the identities that are important to us. As Jane Roscoe (2013) noted, this was the concept of performance of the self brought to life in the everyday conversations of audiences. The river of material that flowed from reality television allowed people to judge and speculate on front stage and back stage performances. Webcams in the *Big Brother* house showed people sleeping, surely a glimpse into an authentic self; cameras caught people arguing, perhaps an unguarded self in an emotional situation; edited programmes represented people trying to be too nice or too nasty, which could be a forced performance to win viewer votes. John Corner (2002) described these performances in *Big Brother* as selving, inviting judgements from audiences about drama and actuality in reality television.

The mediation process of reality television changed the dynamics of people's performances of the self. At first, in the early days of competitive reality, a performance of the self could be characterized by acting up. Acting up is something audiences associated with trying to present a socially acceptable self, keeping a lid on anger or frustration, wanting to appear in a positive light in front of cameras that would capture a performance of the self and broadcast it to millions. Seventy per cent of respondents claimed people acted up for the cameras in reality TV programmes in 2000, in a representative survey of 8,216 adults in the UK aged 16–65+. At the time, acting up was mainly understood as positive impression management. One male viewer described acting up in reality TV as 'I'd be worse if I wasn't filmed!' (aged 35–50).

Competitive reality pushed the performance of the self into an exaggeration of people's personas. There was an increased confidence in performing multiple selves and social roles, such as being a working-class contestant or being a pop idol. We can trace a transition in reality television from participants acting up and positive impression management of themselves in everyday life to a more exaggerated social role where participants acted out, or played up to the cameras with overt performances. Such a transition in performance of selves was located in two different kinds of spaces in reality television. Participants adopted a quieter performance mode for the 'world' space of banal forms of reality television based in airports, restaurants or hotels, and another more overt performance mode for the 'television' space of competitive reality set in studios or special locations.

Participants as contestants realized that negative attention could be just as valuable as positive attention; the public voted for people they liked and disliked to stay in a competition, and for certain contestants being public hate figures generated a great deal of media interest and offers of work. A performance of selves and social roles in competitive reality formats like *America's Next Top Model* (CW 2003–, USA) became associated with acting out. Misha Kavka (2008, 2012) argues that reality television is an example of acting out, using emotional performances as a means of generating viewers' and users' attention. Stephen Coleman (2010) claims the genre is an example of acting powerfully, using performances of power as acting out, manipulation and domination, creating space for reflections on power and political inequality in society.

The power dynamic surrounding the performance of the self is caught up in the tensions between power as associated with a media system, for example entertainment producers, format owners or executive producers, and power as associated with individual agency, for example participants, viewers and users. Mark Lawson (2012) noted:

> In the same way that newspaper journalists have become used to interviewees joking: 'Have you hacked my phone?', so TV reporters

and producers are now accustomed to their subjects asking: 'You're not going to edit me to make me look stupid, are you?' As viewers have become increasingly sophisticated about the medium, it is now standard suspicion that documentaries are cast and edited like fiction to create a dramatic narrative.

People's knowledge of the mediation processes within reality television means that the power of the performance of selves is fraught with difficulty. For some critics, the media is the power player, driving a dramatic narrative of commercialism. For others, participants and audiences complicate power dynamics; participants can challenge how they have been represented, or audiences can criticize what they see and turn their attention elsewhere. Formats consultant Julie Donovan (2013) reflects: 'The audience is sophisticated, they can anticipate the language of TV before it even happens.'

At this juncture in time, there are at least two dominant performance modes in reality television. The first mode of performance of the self comes from the early years of the genre. We can summarize this mode as about banal moments, the little things in everyday life. Audiences watch and witness and interact with people performing themselves, and catch a glimpse of authenticity within the social drama of reality television. The second, more major mode of performance is about big moments, the tears and tantrums, in the staged reality of entertainment formats. Judge Randy Jackson in *American Idol* (Fox 2012, USA) called this a 'moment's moment'. Producers and participants intervene so that performances became manipulated and softly scripted to exaggerate personalities and emotions. This is a performance of a meta me, formatted for multi-media into bite-sized clips that can be shared, commented on and re-mediated for millions of contemporary audiences and users. These different ways of performing yourself are produced in what Coleman (2010) calls a 'theatre of power'. This is a mediated space were we see the push and pull of power dynamics between producers, participants and audiences.

Gary Carter (2013) reflects on the significance of a performance of the self:

> What is really important about reality television is the performance of the self by participants. This performance is the source of reality television's compulsion for the audience, it is the source of the compulsion to participate amongst those who appear onscreen, and this self performance is significant in terms of where digital technology is taking us. Reality television suggests the way developing forms of technology like the internet become platforms for individual performance. This is what is interestingly and lastingly significant about reality television: its effect is present in all other aspects of electronic media – not just the 'old', but the 'new'.

Douglas Wood (2013) also notes the development of reality television towards a 'connected experience', where a performance of the self shifts across digital media and everyday life, a 'dissolve between the onscreen and the afterscreen'.

We witness performances in all shapes and sizes. Many of these performances borrow from established styles within reality television, for example the trope of talent show audition, from being a nobody to being somebody special. Some are reflexive performances that mix traditional and new styles. For example *Catfish: The TV Show* (MTV 2012–) investigates fake and true identities in online and real-world scenarios. Others are experimental performances, challenging our sense of self. For example, artists like Banksy in *Exit Through The Gift Shop* (2010).

As Carter notes (2013): 'Who am I really on a screen? The day you can smell me, see whether I have and haven't shaved, as that technology develops we are going to question what we can and cannot control about representations in the media.' The question of 'who am I really?' runs through performances of selves in reality television. There is no easy answer to this question. A performance of selves and social roles is a situated process, so exploring this across different media content produces more, not fewer, questions. 'The audience's obsession with reality television is about how real people are, how close to their actual self they are being' (Carter 2013).

The question of 'who is in control?' also dominates debates about reality television. If we follow Stephen Coleman's (2010) discussion of *Big Brother* as a theatre of power then performance becomes caught up in the power dynamics between reality television producers, participants, audiences and users. There are two sides of the debate about who is in control. One argument follows a political, economic and critical media analysis of reality television as commodifying the individual. From this perspective reality television producers and broadcasting executives manipulate the audience's obsession with performance of selves, exploiting the narcissistic culture that critics argue is a feature of late modernity. Acting powerfully in this industry and economic context is an illusion of power, where the commodity value of reality television drives its developments at all costs, regardless of ethics. There is little hesitation about who is in control from this critique of reality television.

The argument put forward here is that there are alternatives to such a starkly negative perspective of reality television. When we consider audiences, the question of who is in control becomes more difficult to answer. Reality television is popular entertainment, and as such offers resources for people in their exploration of identity, agency and power. From this perspective, reality television producers, participants and audiences are engaged in contradictory practices that have a push–pull dynamic. The economics of reality television push audiences, users and consumers into a commericalized world, and at the same time people pull all sorts of meanings and different values from cross-media content. Acting powerfully in this popular cultural context is an example of what power looks like as messy and contradictory practices. There is not one person or agent dominating another, but an inherent ambiguity as to who is in control in reality television.

In this sense, Coleman's description of *Big Brother* as a theatre of power is richly suggestive of the power play of reality television. Who am I really? Who is in control? These are questions that require qualified answers. The ways we perform ourselves in the television space of competitive reality, for example, are different from how we perform ourselves in the mediated space of the internet, or the private space of the home. As McGrath (2004) notes, we are selves producing selves for different audiences in multiple settings. This play off between power, performance and authenticity drives developments within reality television and its influence on popular culture.

PRODUCING AUTHENTICITY

Much of this concluding chapter has focused on the momentum of reality television to go towards entertainment, performance and spectacle. The popularity of competitive reality, talent formats and structured reality television has overemphasized a spectacle of excess. Such a development in reality television reduces our connection with the ordinary and the deeply mundane. A return to the authentic seems a strange way to end the chapter. And yet, reality TV has gone so far towards entertainment that it has come full circle, returning to some of the original questions of authenticity it addressed in early forms of infotainment or popular factual entertainment. Jane Roscoe (2013) comments: 'People want to get back to something more authentic. It sounds odd, as no TV show is authentic, but that is an interesting dynamic producing authenticity.'

Authenticity is a tricky term, as it can mean something is an original, the one and only, or a copy of an original, an authentic replica. The very term demands alertness. According to Gary Carter (2013), there is:

a sense of slipperiness in modern society about what is real. Rather than embracing what is *not* real, we have become really, really obsessed with what *is* real – as if we know. We make these claims to authenticity as if we know what authenticity is.

In 'The Bogus Quest for Authentic Food', blogger Sejal Sukhadwala (2012) commented: 'Barely a day goes by without a restaurant, cookery book or TV chef shouting about their "authenticity" credentials. But what on earth is "authentic" food, and most importantly, does it taste better?' There are authentic leadership courses. 'Discovering your authentic leadership requires a commitment to developing yourself. Like musicians and athletes, you must devote yourself to a lifetime of realizing your potential' (George *et al.* 2007). As Roscoe notes: 'everything has got to be authentic now' (2013).

Reality television has always been about the slippery side of reality. It has never made grand truth claims. And yet it can offer reflections on reality if audiences 'take it with a pinch of salt'. In some ways the mediation process of reality television lends itself to a questioning of realism. In competitive reality or talent shows the drive is more towards a manufactured moment, but in other kinds of series there is a rougher, more authentic feel to representations of reality. Roscoe (2013) comments:

We have gone as far as we can with reality TV to the point where the fixed rig shows can capture every single moment. We seem to have been everywhere, hospitals, babies being born, schools, custody units, you have gone as far as you can. So where do you go back from that? People are talking about different ways to engage with emotional authenticity. It feels, from an industry point of view, that whilst those fixed rig shows will continue, people are looking at different ways of telling real stories.

An executive producer of reality television in Denmark commented on how they were taking a different perspective on producing reality. Mistakes, out-takes, a presenter stumbling over words, a participant doing something unexpected – this is what they were looking for in production. Just a few years ago this rougher, less manufactured performance would have been edited out of the picture. Here, we see the ways reality television producers find an alternative to the manufactured moment. Not polishing reality so it is reduced to one-liners, but opening up a connection with the ordinary again.

Educating Yorkshire (Channel 4 2013, UK) is one example of mixing documentary and reality styles of filming to produce authenticity. The series is a 'development out of the observational documentary of the 1970s and 1980s, with an inflection towards reality television expectations but a commitment to mundane institutional realism' (Corner 2014). The series was nominated as a factual series in the BAFTA 2014 awards. Although it has documentary sensibilities, in the crafting of each episode as a one-off, it borrows from reality television in capturing every banal moment on camera:

It is about those little everyday banalities – I've shaved off all my eyebrows, brilliant. The girl that thought letters and numbers were the same thing, brilliant ... Each episode is thematically structured, tightly edited, there is no chaff in there. That gives viewers a much better experience. 'I am watching real people, you can tell it is not scripted, you couldn't script half of that.' But it is tightly made and produced.

(Roscoe 2013)

Roscoe (2013) commented that 'people may not say it is a search for the authentic but to me it is about that. How do we get unguarded moments to fill in the emotional terrain?'

The popularity of drama, offering emotional engagement through the performance and staging of an historical event, is another example of producing authenticity. There are drama series loosely based on historical accounts of building the railroads in nineteenth-century America (*Hell on Wheels*, AMC 2011–) or criminal gangs after the First World War in Birmingham (*Peaky Blinders*, BBC2 2013). Films such as *12 Years a Slave* (director Steve McQueen 2014) are based on the memoir of Solomon Northup; even though the memoir is open to debate as to its historical accuracy, the account offers an emotional truth to what is thought to be an authentic experience.

In the novel *Elegy for April* by Benjamin Black (2012) the character of Inspector Hackett reflects on reality: 'The world, he was sure, was never what it seemed, was always more than it appeared to be. He had learned that early on. To take reality as it presented itself was to miss an entirely other reality hidden behind' (2012: 112). Reality TV is an inter-generic space for reflection on multiple realities. Live events, programmes and formats invite audiences to riff on reality, to debate and reject reality claims. 'Maybe one of the reasons why we find it so gripping is that it does raise the question we already ask ourselves – what is real?' (Carter 2013).

Here are some viewers talking about reality TV:

Karen: There's something about people who willingly volunteer themselves to be seen, sort of ... They put themselves forward as something to be looked at. Maybe that's a feature of reality TV. (56-year-old female librarian)

John: I don't know. Because they know that they are filmed,
         I don't know how real that is ... I don't know, do
         they really have the same reactions if they know
         they're filmed by a lot of cameras? And there are two,
         three, four, ten million people watching? I don't
         know. (41-year-old male financial consultant)

Brenda: But people are faking anyway. So I suppose every time
         it is real. Even if you know that they don't react like
         they do, it's like this in life. Even pretending to be
         something is real. Even if you cannot understand why,
         you can understand more, even if it's acting what
         you're seeing. (40-year-old female property developer)

John: Yes, but, when you know the day after the newspapers
         will talk about you? I don't know.

Brenda: Yeah, exactly, you see exactly how people are thinking
         of celebrity, of the news, these come up after you see
         it. And that's something that's real. It reflects the
         time. It happens. It reflects a whole system.

In this book we have listened to audiences talk about reality television as popular entertainment, the play off between performance and authenticity and its connections to a social and media
matrix. In short, how reality TV 'reflects the time', how it
'reflects a whole system'.

APPENDIX

The first data set comes from the British Film Institute Audience Tracking Study, which contained a sample that was generally representative of the population as a whole. This was a long-itudinal study designed to run from 1991–96 and consisted of 15 questionnaire diaries completed by an initial 509 respondents, which had dropped to 427 respondents at the end of the project. The aims of this project were related to everyday live and television in transition. There was some data in this project on reality TV (see Hill 2000b).

The second data set includes research from 2000–1 in Britain. This project was about reality TV audiences and contained a survey distributed by the Broadcasters' Audience Research Board (BARB) to a representative sample of 8,216 adults (16–65+) and 937 children (4–15) during August 2000; 12 semi-structured focus groups (7–8 participants), with children (aged 11–14), young adults (aged 15–18) and adults (aged 18–44), who defined themselves as regular viewers of popular factual television, and were in the C1C2DE social category (lower-middle class and working class), during 2000–1; in-depth interviews with ten families, with children of varying ages, over a six-month period in 2001, living in the Greater London area and in the C1C2DE social categories.

A third data set comes from 2003–4. This project was about audiences for factual television, from news and documentary to reality TV. The data included a quantitative survey with a representative sample of 4,516 British people aged 16–65+, carried out by Ipsos RSL. In Sweden a quantitative survey was conducted with a random sample of 2,000 people, in co-operation with the SOM Institute, Göteborg University, and carried out by Kinnmark Information AB. The net sample was 1,854 people, with 944 respondents and a net response rate of 51 per cent. The distribution amongst responses compared with the Swedish population as a whole, and also compared with another representative survey (National SOM study 2004). During 2003–4 a series of semi-structured focus groups were conducted in Sweden and Britain. There were 24 groups, 12 in each country, with a total of 129 respondents aged 18–60. The sample was based on the criteria of age (roughly split into two groups of 20–30 year olds, and 40–60 year olds), gender (even mix of male and female) and socio-economic status (working and middle class, and educational levels from school to university).

A fourth data set is taken from a longitudinal study of media and interactivity in 30 households in the Greater London area (2005–7). This involved in-depth interviews with 27 households involving 70 participants. The aim of this project was to examine media interactivity, including television, mobile and internet design. Questions on reality TV were a secondary part of the project, relating to reality TV formats and interactive elements like voting, the internet and mobile applications. The fifth data set is from 2007–8. This project was about audiences for the paranormal in popular culture, and included a case study of reality TV and its representations of ghosts, alternative medicine and extraordinary people and their experiences. Over 100 men and women aged 18–65+ took part in focus group interviews.

A final data set is part of an on-going project on reality TV and audience experiences, starting in 2013 and continuing until 2016. This data includes social media analytics, from Twitter and other websites and micro blogs, press reports, industry interviews with professionals, industry data on audiences, interviews, focus groups and participant observation. The sample includes men and women, aged 16–65+, in Britain, Sweden and Denmark. It is funded by the Wallenbergs Foundation, Sweden, and conducted in collaboration with Shine Group.

REFERENCES

Abercrombie, Nick and Longhurst, Brian. (1998) *Audiences: A Sociological Theory of Performance and Imagination*, London: Sage.

Ackerman, Diane. (1995) *A Natural History of the Senses*, London: Vintage.

Ahmed, Sara. (2004) 'Affective Economies' *Social Text*, 22(2): 117–39.

Ahtola, Dan. (2012) 'Interview with Author', November 2012.

——(2013) 'Interview with Author', March 2013.

Aitkenhead, Decca. (2014) 'Deirdre Kelly, AKA White Dee: I Would Never Watch a show called Benefits Street' *Guardian*, Saturday Interview, 8 March.

Allen, Robert C. (1985) *Speaking of Soap Operas*, North Carolina: North Carolina University Press.

——(2008) 'Going to the Show' conference paper, ECREA, November 2008, University of Barcelona. Also see 'Going to the Show' history of moviegoing project at official website: www.docsouth.unc.edu/gtts.

Altman, Rick (ed.). (1992) *Sound Theory Sound Practice*, London and New York: Routledge.

Andrejevic, Mark. (2004) *Reality TV: The Work of Being Watched*, Maryland: Rowman and Littlefield.

——(2009) 'Visceral Literacy: Reality TV, Savvy Viewers, and Auto-Spies', in S. Murray and L. Ouellette (eds) *Reality TV: Remaking Television Culture*, New York: New York University Press: 321–42.

Ball, Michael. (1990) *Professional Wrestling as Ritual Drama in American Popular Culture*, Lewiston, NY: Edwin Mellen Press.

Barthes, Roland. (1957, 1972) *Mythologies*, New York: Hill and Wang Publishers.

Baudrillard, Jean. (1995) 'The Virtual Illusion: Or the Automatic Writing of the World', *Theory, Culture and Society* (12): 97.

Bazalgette, Peter. (2005) *Billion Dollar Game: How Three Men Risked it all and Changed the Face of Television*, London: Time Warner Books.

BBC. (2011) 'Today Show', Radio Four, 25 May.

——(2013) 'Official blog *The Voice*, season two', 22 June. Accessed online: www.bbc.co.uk/blogs/thevoiceuk/authors/_The_Voice_James.

Becker, Karin, Kautsky, Robert and Widholm, Andreas. (2014) 'Watching Football in the Fan Park: Mediatization, Spectatorship and Fan Identity', in L. Duits, K. Zwaan and S. Reijnders (eds) *The Ashgate Research Companion to Fan Cultures*, Surrey: Ashgate.

Beekman, Scott M. (2006) *Ringside: A History of Professional Wrestling in America*, Westport: Praeger Publishers.

Bennington, Emily. (2010) 'Does Reality TV Make Us Stupid?', *Huffington Post*, 15 May. Accessed online: www.huffingtonpost.com/emily-bennington/does-reality-tv-make-us-s_b_496084.html.

Bethell, Andrew. (1999) 'A Job, Some Stars and a Big Row', *Sight and Sound*: *Mediawatch*, 99(3): 14–15.

Bignell, Jonathan. (2005) *Big Brother: Reality TV in the Twenty-first Century*, Basingstoke: Palgrave Macmillan.

Billington, Michael. (2014) 'I Can't Sing Review', *Guardian*, 26 March.

Biltereyst, Daniel. (2003) 'Reality TV, Troublesome Pictures and Panics: Reappraising the Public Controversy Around Reality TV in Europe', in S. Holmes and D. Jermyn, *Understanding Reality Television*, London: Routledge: 91–110.

Biressi, Anita and Nunn, Heather. (2005) *Reality TV*, London: Wallflower Press.

Black, Benjamin. (2012) *Elegy for April*, London: Mantle.

Bolin, Göran. (2011) *Value and the Media: Cultural Production and Consumption in Digital Markets*, London: Ashgate.

Bonner, Frances. (2003) *Ordinary Television*, London: Sage.

Boyle, Raymond and Haynes, Richard. (2009) *Power Play: Sport, the Media and Popular Culture*, 2nd edition, Edinburgh: Edinburgh University Press.

Boyle, Raymond and Kelly, Lisa. (2012) *The Television Entrepreneurs*, Surrey: Ashgate.

Brache, Ruben. (2013) *Guardian* forum, 25 March, 11:36am. Accessed online: www.guardian.co.uk/discussion/user/id/10689372 (accessed 25 March 2013).

Brants, Kees. (1998) 'Who's Afraid of Infotainment', *European Journal of Communication*, 13(3): 315–35.

Brooker, Charlie. (2012) 'The Cast of Geordie Shore are the Noblest People in Britain Today', *Guardian*, 1 July 2012.

Brown, Maggie. (2005) 'The Knives are Out', *Guardian*, Media Section, 18 April: 10–11.

——(2014) 'Sofa Stars of Gogglebox Go Primetime', *Observer*, 23 February. Accessed online: www.theguardian.com/tv-and-radio/2014/feb/23/goggleboxturns-viewers-into-tv-stars-channel-4.

Brunsdon, Charlotte, Johnson, Catherine, Moseley, Rachel and Wheatley, Helen. (2001) 'Factual Entertainment on British Television: The Midlands TV Research Group's "8–9 Project"', *European Journal of Cultural Studies*, 4(1): 29–62.

Calhoun, Craig and Sennett, Richard (eds). (2007) *Practicing Cultures*, London: Routledge.

Calvert, Clay. (2000) *Voyeur Nation: Media, Privacy, and Peering in Modern Culture*, Boulder, CO: Westview Press.

Cantrell, Tom and Luckhurst, Mary. (2010) *Playing for Real: Actors on Playing Real People*, London: Palgrave Macmillan.

Carpentier, Nico. (2011) *Media and Participation: A Site of Ideological-Democratic Struggle*, Bristol: Intellect.

Carter, Bill. (2013) '"Walking Dead" premiere is Highest Rated Show of TV Season', *The New York Times*, 14 October. Accessed online: www.nytimes.com/2013/10/15/business/media/walking-dead-premiere-is-highest-rated-show-of-tv-season.html.

——(2014) 'Once a Hit, its Ratings Make "Idol" An Also-Ran', *The New York Times*, 21 March. Accessed online: www.nytimes.com/2014/03/22/business/media/once-a-juggernaut-american-idol-becomes-a-ratings-also-ran.html.

Carter, Gary. (2013) 'Interview with Author', 20 November 2013.

——(2014) 'Comments to Author', 19 May 2014.

Cashmore, Ellis. (2004) *Beckham*, Cambridge: Polity.

Claessens, Nathalie and Van den Bulck, Hilde. (2014) 'A Severe Case of Disliking Bimbo Heidi, Scumbag Jesse and Bastard Tiger: Analyzing Celebrities' Online Anti-fans' in L. Duits, K. Zwaan and S. Reijnders (eds) *The Ashgate Research Companion to Fan Cultures*, London: Ashgate.

Coleman, Stephen. (2010) 'Acting Powerfully: Performances of Power in *Big Brother*', *International Journal of Cultural Studies*, 13(2): 127–46.

Coleman, Stephen and Ross, Karen. (2010) *The Media and the Public*, London: Wiley and Sons.

Corner, John. (1992) 'Presumption as Theory: "Realism" in Television Studies', *Screen*, 33(1): 97–102.

——(1996) *The Art of Record: A Critical Introduction to Documentary*, Manchester: Manchester University Press.

——(2002) 'Performing the Real', *Television and New Media*, 3(3): 255–69.

——(2009) 'Performing the Real: Documentary Diversions (with Afterword)' in S. Murray and L. Ouellette (eds) *Reality TV: Remaking Television Culture*, New York: New York University Press: 44–64.

——(2011) *Theorising Media: Power, Form and Subjectivity*, Manchester: Manchester University Press.

——(2014) 'Comments to Author', 25 May 2014.

Couldry, Nick. (2010) *Why Voice Matters*, London: Sage.

——(2011) 'Making Populations Appear', in M. Kraidy and K. Sender (eds) *The Politics of Reality Television: Global Perspectives*, London and New York: Routledge.

Dahlgren, Peter. (2009) *Media and Political Engagement: Citizens, Communication, and Democracy*, Cambridge: Cambridge University Press.

Daily Mail. (2013) '*Splash!* Becomes our TV Guilty Pleasure', 16 January. Accessed online: www.dailymail.co.uk/news/article-2263117/Splash-TV-guilty-pleasure-figures-watched-programme-Saturday-night.html.

Deery, June. (2012) *Consuming Reality: The Commercialization of Factual Entertainment*, New York: Palgrave Macmillan.

Delwiche, Aaron and Jacobs Henderson, Jennifer (eds). (2013) *The Participatory Cultures Handbook*, New York: Routledge.

Dent, Grace. (2013) 'Grace Dent on TV: Gogglebox, Channel 4', 11 October. Accessed online: www.independent.co.uk/arts-entertainment/tv/reviews/grace-dent-on-tv-gogglebox-channel-4-8872137.html.

Deuze, Mark. (2012) *Media Life*, London: Polity.

Donovan, Julie. (2013) 'Interview with Author', 16 August 2013.

Dover, Caroline and Hill, Annette. (2007) 'Mapping Genres' in D. Heller (ed.) *Makeover Television*, London and New York: IB Taurus: 23–38.

Dovey, Jon. (2000) *Freakshows: First Person Media and Factual Television*, London: Pluto.

Duits, Linda, Zwaan, Koos and Reijnders, Stijn (eds). (2014) *The Ashgate Research Companion to Fan Cultures*, London: Ashgate.

Elias, Norbert and Dunning, Eric. (1986) *The Quest for Excitement: Sport and Leisure in the Civilizing Process*, New York: Basil Blackwell.

Faulks, Sebastian. (2009) *A Week in December*, London: Vintage.

Ford, Sam. (2014) '10 Things Corporations Can Learn From Pro Wrestling', www.fastcompany.com.

Forster, Derek. (2004) '"Jump in the Pool": The competitive culture of *Survivor* fan networks', in S. Holmes and D. Jermyn (eds) *Understanding Reality Television*, London: Routledge: 270–89.

FremantleMedia. (2014) *Idols*. Accessed online: www.fremantlemedia.com/Production/Our_brands/Idols.aspx.

Gallagher, William. (2000) 'The Year of Reality TV', *BBC News*, 23 December. Accessed online: http://news.bbc.co.uk/1/hi/entertainment/1083109.stm.

Gauntlett, David and Hill, Annette. (1999) *TV Living*, London: Routledge.

George, Bill, Sims, Peter, McLean, Andrew and Mayer, Diana. (2007) 'Discovering Your Authentic Leadership', *Harvard Business Review*. Accessed online: http://hbr.org/2007/02/discovering-your-authentic-leadership/ar/1.

Giuffre, Liz. (2014) 'Music for (Something Other Than) Pleasure: Anti-fans and the Other Side of Popular Music Appeal' in L. Duits, K. Zwaan and S. Reijnders (eds) (2014) *The Ashgate Research Companion to Fan Cultures*, London: Ashgate.

Glynn, Kevin. (2000) *Tabloid Culture: Trash Taste, Popular Power, and the Transformation of American Television*, Durham and London: Duke University Press.

Goffman, Erving. (1959) *The Presentation of Self in Everyday Life*, Harmondsworth: Penguin Books.

Gray, Jonathan. (2003) 'New Audiences, New Textualities: Anti-Fans and Non-Fans', *International Journal of Cultural Studies*, 6(1): 64–81.

Gray, Jonathan, Sandvoss, Cornel and Harrington, C. Lee. (eds). (2007) *Fandom: Identities and Communities in a Mediated World*, New York: New York University Press.

Griffen-Foley, Bridget. (2004) 'From Tit-Bits to Big Brother: A Century of Audience Participation in the Media', *Media, Culture and Society*, 26(4): 533–48.

Grindstaff, Laura. (2011) 'Just Be Yourself – Only More So: Ordinary Celebrity in the Era of Self-Service Television' in M. Kraidy and K. Sender (eds) (2011) *The Politics of Reality Television: Global Perspectives*, London and New York: Routledge: 44–58.

Guardian. (2011) 'Blog posts', 9 August. Accessed online: www.theguardian.com/tv-and-radio/tvandradioblog/2011/aug/09/the-only-way-is-essex.

Hall, Stuart. (2011) 'The Neo-liberal Revolution', *Cultural Studies*, 25(6): 705–28.

Halperin, Shirley. (2013) '"American Idol" Finale's Ratings Free Fall: What Went Wrong', *The Hollywood Reporter*, 17 May. Accessed online: www.hollywoodreporter.com/idol-worship/american-idol-finales-ratings-free-524775.

Hawley, Chris. (2009) 'World Wrestling Entertainment has Lucha Libre on the Ropes', *USA Today*, 30 December. Accessed online: http://usatoday30.usatoday.com/news/offbeat/2009-12-29-lucha-libre_N.htm (accessed 7 April 2014).

Hearn, Alison. (2009) 'Hoaxing the "Real": On the Metanarrative of Reality Television', in S. Murray and L. Ouellette (eds) *Reality TV: Remaking Television Culture*, New York: New York University Press: 165–78.

Henricks, Thomas. (1974) 'Professional Wrestling as Moral Order', *Sociological Inquiry*, 44(3): 177–88.

Heritage, Stuart. (2012) 'Why Full Metal Jousting Is my Programme of the Year', *Guardian*, 19 December. Accessed online: www.guardian.co.uk/tv-and-radio/video/2012/dec/19/full-metal-jousting-tv-video (accessed 19 December 2012).

——(2013a) 'Slow TV', *Guardian*, 4 October. Accessed online: www.theguardian.com/tv-and-radio/tvandradioblog/2013/oct/04/slow-tv-norwegian-movement-nrk.

——(2013b) 'The Voice final 2013: live blog', *Guardian*, 22 June. Accessed online: www.theguardian.com/tv-and-radio/tvandradioblog/2013/jun/22/the-voice-final-2013-live-blog.

——(2013c) 'Why Tom Daley's Splash! Can't Bellyflop,' *Guardian*, 4 January. Accessed online: www.theguardian.com/tv-and-radio/tvandradioblog/2013/jan/04/tom-daley-splash-bellyflop.

Herman, James. (2012) 'American Idol Castoff Joshua Ledet Talks Favourite Moments', *The Hollywood Reporter*, 18 May 2012. Accessed online: http://www.hollywoodreporter.com/magazine/may-18-2012.

Hermes, Joke. (1995) *Reading Women's Magazines*, London: Polity.

——(2005) *Re-reading Popular Culture*, London: Blackwell.

——(2012) 'The Scary Promise of Technology: Developing New Forms of Audience Research' in G. Bolin (ed.) *Cultural Technologies: The Shaping of Culture in Media and Society*, New York: Routledge: 189–201.

Hibberd, James. (2013a) '"Splash" Finale Ratings Just a Drop in the Bucket', *Entertainment Weekly*, 8 May. Accessed online: http://insidetv.ew.com/2013/05/08/splash-finale-ratings-just-a-drop-in-the-bucket/.

——(2013b) '"The Walking Dead": How to Comprehend its Massive Ratings', *Entertainment Weekly*, 11 November. Accessed online: http://insidetv.ew.com/2013/11/11/the-walking-dead-ratings/.

Hill, Annette. (2000a) 'Crime and Crisis: British Reality TV in Action', in E. Buscombe (ed.) *British Television: A Reader*, Oxford: Oxford University Press.

——(2000b) 'Fearful and Safe: Audience Response to British Reality Programming', *Television and New Media*, 1(2), May 2000: 193–214.

——(2002) '*Big Brother*: The Real Audience', *Television and New Media*, 3(3): 323–40.

——(2004) 'Watching *Big Brother* UK', in E. Mathjis and J. Jones (eds) *Big Brother International: Formats, Critics and Publics*, London: Wallflower Press: 25–39.

——(2005) *Reality TV: Audiences and Popular Factual Television*, London: Routledge.

——(2007) *Restyling Factual TV: Audiences and News, Documentary and Reality Genres*, London: Routledge.

——(2011) *Paranormal Media: Audiences, Spirits and Magic in Popular Culture*, London: Routledge.

——(2012) 'Audiences in the Round' in K. B. Jensen (ed.) *The Handbook of Media and Communication Research*, London: Routledge: 302–17.

Hill, Annette and Palmer, Gareth. (2002) '*Big Brother*: Special Issue', *Television and New Media*, 3(3), August 2002.

Hill, Annette and Steemers, Jeanette. (2011) 'Big Formats. Small Nations: Does Size Matter?' in G. Lowe, C, Nilsson and R. Picard (eds) *Why Size Matters*, Gothenberg: Nordicom.

Hill, Annette, Weibull, Lennart and Nilsson, Åsa. (2005) *Audiences and Factual and Reality Television in Sweden*, JIBS Research Reports No. 2005-4, Jönköping: JIBS.

——(2006) 'Public and Popular: British and Swedish Audience Trends in Factual and Reality Television', *Cultural Trends*, 16(1): 17–42.

Hills, Matt. (2002) *Fan Cultures*, London: Routledge.

Hjarvard, Stig. (2013) *The Mediatization of Culture and Society*, London: Routledge.

Hobson, Dorothy. (2003) *Soap Opera*, Oxford: Wiley Blackwell.

Hochschild, Arlie. (2003) *The Commercialization of Intimate Life: Notes from Home and Work*, Berkeley: University of California Press.

Hollender, Pål. (2014) 'Interview with Author', 14 April 2014.

The Hollywood Reporter. (2012) 'THR's Reality TV Poll: The 6 Biggest Surprises', 16 May. Accessed online: www.hollywoodreporter.com/gallery/thrs-reality-tv-poll-6-324799.

Holmes, Su. (2010) 'Reality TV and "Ordinary" People: Re-visiting Celebrity, Performance, and Authenticity', in S. Van Bauwel and N. Carpentier (eds) (2010) *Trans-Reality Television: The Trangression of Reality, Genre, Politics, and Audience*, Plymouth: Lexington Books: 251–74.

Holmes, Su and Jermyn, Deborah. (2004) *Understanding Reality Television*, London: Routledge.

Household, N. (1998) 'Alder Hey – It's Been a Privilege', *Radio Times*, 30 May–5 June: 27–28.

Hyde, Marina. (2009) 'Reality TV is Not Dead: The End of *Big Brother* Marks its Coming of Age', *Guardian*, 28 August. Accessed online: www.theguardian.com/commentisfree/2009/aug/28/big-brother-reality-simon-cowell (accessed 14 November 2013).

Imre, Anikó. (2011) 'Love to Hate: National Celebrity and Racial Intimacy on Reality TV in the New Europe', *Television and New Media*, 2011: 1–28.

James, William. (1896) 'The Will to Believe', address to the Philosophical Clubs of Yale and Brown Universities (published in *New World*, June 1896).

Jenkins, Henry. (2009) 'Buying into *American Idol*: How We Are Being Sold on Reality Television', in S. Murray and L. Ouellette (eds) *Reality TV: Remaking Television Culture*, New York: New York University Press: 343–62.

Johnson, Angella. (2013) '"I Made Big Brother And I'm Your New Arts Chief ... Get Over It!" Peter Bazalgette's Mission to Inform, Entertain and Infuriate', *Daily Mail*. Accessed online: www.dailymail.co.uk/news/article-2283441/I-Big-Brother-AND-Im-new-arts-chief--GET-OVER-IT-Peter-Bazalgettes-mission-inform-entertain-infuriate.html#ixzz31R3YJksv.

Kaufman, Seth. (2012) *The King of Pain*, New York: Sukuma Books.

——(2013) 'What We Write About When We Write About Reality TV', *Huffington Post*, 15 January. Accessed online: www.huffingtonpost.com/seth-kaufman/what-we-write-about-when-b_2474548.html.

Kavka, Misha. (2008) *Reality Television, Affect and Intimacy*, London and New York: Palgrave Macmillan.

——(2012) *Reality TV*, Edinburgh: Edinburgh University Press.

Kavka, Misha and West, Amy. (2004) 'Temporalities of the Real: Conceptualising Time in Reality TV' in S. Holmes and D. Jermyn (eds) *Understanding Reality Television*, London: Routledge: 136–53.

Kerrick, George, E. (1980) 'The Jargon of Professional Wrestling', *American Speech*, 55(2) (Summer, 1980). Accessed online: www.jstor.org/stable/3050508 (accessed 2 April 2014).

Kilborn, Richard. (1994) "How Real Can You Get?": Recent Developments in "Reality" Television', *European Journal of Communication*, 9(4): 421–39.

——(2003) *Staging the Real: Factual TV Programming in the Age of* Big Brother, Manchester: Manchester University Press.

Kraidy, Marwan and Sender, Katherine (eds). (2011) *The Politics of Reality Television: Global Perspectives*, London and New York: Routledge.

Lawson, Mark. (2012) '*The Choir*: Is Discord over Editing Justified?' *Guardian*, 14 September. Accessed online: www.theguardian.com/tv-and-radio/tvandradio-blog/2012/sep/14/gareth-malone-choir-editing.

——(2014) '*I Can't Sing!* to *The Hunger Games*: How Reality TV Broke Out of the Box', *Guardian*, 30 March. Accessed online: www.theguardian.com/stage/2014/mar/27/i-cant-sing-the-hunger-games-reality-tv-harry-hill.

Le Carré, John. (1993) *The Night Manager*, London: Hodder and Stoughton.

Lehane, Dennis. (2010) *Moonlight Mile*, Boston: Sphere Publications.

Levi, Heather. (1998) 'Lean Mean Fighting Queens: Drag in the World of Mexican Professional Wrestling', *Sexualities*, 1(3): 275–85.

——(2008) *The World of Lucha Libre: Secrets, Revelations, and Mexican National Identity*, Durham, NC: Duke University Press.

Lindsay, Jeff. (2010) *Dexter is Delicious*, London: Orion.

Lipkin, Steve, N. (2002) *Real Emotional Logic: Film and Television Docudrama as Persuasive Practice*, Carbondale and Edwardsville: Southern Illinois University Press.

Lippman, Laura. (2000) *The Sugar House*, New York: Harper Collins.

Livingstone, Sonia and Lunt, Peter. (1994) *Talk on Television: Audience Participation and Public Debate*, London: Routledge.

Lunt, Peter. (2009) *Stanley Milgram: Understanding Obedience and its Implications*, London: Palgrave Macmillan.

Lunt, Peter and Stenner, Paul. (2005) '*The Jerry Springer Show* as an Emotional Public Sphere', *Media, Culture and Society*, 27(1): 59–81.

Lury, Karen. (2005) *Interpreting Television*, London: Hodder Arnold.

McCarthy, Anna. (2009) '"Stanley Milgram, Allen Fun, and Me": Postwar Social Science and the "First Wave" of Reality TV', in S. Murray and L. Ouellette (eds) *Reality TV: Remaking Television Culture*, New York: New York University Press: 23–43.

McGrath, John, E. (2004) *Loving Big Brother: Performance, Privacy and Surveillance Space*, London: Routledge.

Maguire, Brendan. (2005) 'American Professional Wrestling: Evolution, Content, and Popular Appeal', *Sociological Spectrum*, 25(2): 155–76.

Mathijs, Ernest. (2002) 'Big Brother and Critical Discourse', *Television and New Media*, 3(3): 311–22.

Mathijs, Ernest and Jones, Janet (eds). (2004) *Big Brother International: Format, Critics and Publics*, London: Wallflower Press.

Mayer, Vicki. (2011) *Below the Line*, Durham, NC: Duke University Press.

Mazer, Sharon. (1998) *Professional Wrestling: Sport and Spectacle*. Jackson: University of Mississippi Press.

Meyrowitz, Joshua. (1985) *No Sense of Place: The Impact of Electronic Media on Social Behavior*, Oxford: Oxford University Press.

Mikos, Lothar. (2004) '*Big Brother* as Television Text: Frames of Interpretation and Reception in Germany', in E. Mathjis and J. Jones (eds) *Big Brother International: Formats, Critics and Publics*, London: Wallflower Press: 93–104.

Mikos, Lothar, Feise, Patricia, Herzog, Katja, Prommer, Elizabeth and Veihl, Verena. (2000) *Im Auge der Kamera: Das Fernsehereignis Big Brother*, Berlin: Vistas.

Moran, Albert and Malbon, Justin. (2012) *Understanding the Global TV Format*, Bristol: Intellect Books.

Murray, Susan and Ouellette, Laurie (eds). (2004) *Reality TV: Remaking Television Culture*, New York: New York University Press.

——(2009) *Reality TV: Remaking Television Culture*, second edition. New York: New York University Press.

Napoli, Philip. (2010) *Audience Evolution*, New York: Columbia University Press.

Neale, Steve. (1980) *Genre*, London: British Film Institute.

Nelson, Scott A. (1989) 'Crime-Time Television', *FBI Law Enforcement Bulletin*, August 1989: 5.

Nichols, Bill. (1994) *Blurred Boundaries: Questions of Meaning in Contemporary Culture*, Bloomington, IN: Indiana University Press.

Norris, Chris. (2012) 'How Reality Television Shapes Travel', *Travel and Leisure*, February. Accessed online: www.travelandleisure.com/articles/how-reality-television-shapes-travel.

O'Connell, Michael. (2012) 'Sorry, "Honey Boo Boo," the Kardashians Are Still Reality's Reigning Family', *The Hollywood Reporter*, 17 September. Accessed online: www.hollywoodreporter.com/live-feed/here-comes-honey-boo-boo-keeping-up-kardashians-ratings-370856.

——(2014) 'TV Ratings: "Duck Dynasty" Finale Ticks Up, Beats All But "Modern Family"', *The Hollywood Reporter*, 27 March. Accessed online: www.hollywoodreporter.com/live-feed/tv-ratings-duck-dynasty-finale-691686.

Oren, Tasha and Shahaf, Sharon. (2012) *Global Television Formats*, New York: Routledge.

Orwell, George. (1949) *1984*, London: Penguin Books.

Ouellette, Laurie (ed.). (2014) *A Companion to Reality Television*, New Jersey: Wiley Blackwell.

Paget, Derek. (1987) '"Verbatim Theatre": Oral History and Documentary Techniques', *New Theatre Quarterly*, 3(12): 317–36.

——(1998) *No Other Way to Tell It*, Manchester: Manchester University Press.

Paget, Derek and Roscoe, Jane. (2006) 'Giving Voice Performance and Authenticity in the Documentary Musical', *Jump Cut: A Review of Contemporary Media*, 48,

Winter. Accessed online: www.ejumpcut.org/archive/jc48.2006/MusicalDocy/text.html (accessed 19 June 2012).

Palahniuk, Chuck. (2005) *Haunted*, New York: Doubleday.

——(2013) *Doomed*, New York: Doubleday.

Palmer, Gareth. (2003) *Discipline and Liberty*, Manchester: Manchester University Press.

Petridis, Alexis. (2014) 'Harry Hill: Now Giving His X Factor Musical 110%', *Guardian*, 23 February.

Piazza, Jo. (2011) 'Towns and Tourist Sites Get a Bump on Success of TV Shows' Fox News, 26 September. Accessed online: www.FoxNews.com (accessed 3 July 2013).

Pine, Joseph and Gilmore, James. (1999, 2011) *The Experience Economy* (updated edition), Boston: Harvard Business Review.

Plunkett, John. (2013) 'Channel 4 Hit Show Gogglebox Goes Global', *Guardian*, 17 December. Accessed online: www.theguardian.com/media/2013/dec/17/channel-4-gogglebox-goes-global.

Poniewozik, James. (2013) 'Here are 10 of the Worst Things TV Did This Year', *Time*, 17 December. Accessed online: http://entertainment.time.com/2013/12/17/here-are-10-of-the-worst-things-tv-did-this-year/.

Powell, R and Solomon, H. (1992) 'Real to Reel', *Broadcast*, 9 April: 32.

Press Association. (2014) 'X Factor Musical *I Can't Sing!* to Close After Less Than Two Months', *Guardian*, 27 April.

Price, Gareth. (2014) 'Decoding Benefits Street: How Britain was Divided by a Television Show', *Guardian*, 22 February.

Raeside, Julia. (2011a) 'A Different Kind of Reality TV', *Guardian*, 1 June.

——(2011b) 'Today Show', Radio Four, 25 May 2011.

Raffel, Stanley. (2013) 'The Everyday Life of the Self: Reworking Early Goffman', *Journal of Classical Sociology*, February, 13(1): 163–78.

Raphael, Chad. (1997, 2009) 'The Political Economic Origins of Reali-TV' in S. Murray and L. Ouellette (eds) *Reality TV: Remaking Television Culture*, New York: New York University Press: 123–40.

Redhead, Steve. (2014) '"We're Not Racist, We Only Hate Mancs": Post-Subculture and Football Fandom', in L. Duits, K. Zwaan and S. Reijnders (eds) (2014) *The Ashgate Research Companion to Fan Cultures*, London: Ashgate.

Rojek, Chris. (2001) *Celebrity*, London: Reaktion Books.

Roscoe, Jane. (2001) '*Big Brother* Australia: Performing the "Real" Twenty-four-Seven', *International Journal of Cultural Studies*, 4(4): 473–88.

——(2013) 'Interview with Author', 29 November 2013.

Rowe, David and Baker, Stephanie Alice. (2012) '"Truly a Fan Experience"? The Cultural Politics of the Live Site', in R. Krøvel and T. Roksvold (eds) *We Love to Hate Each Other: Mediated Football Fan Culture*. Göteborg: Nordicom.

Sandvoss, Cornel. (2005) *Fans*, Cambridge: Polity.

Sassoon, Donald. (2006) *The Culture of the Europeans: From 1800 to the Present*, London: Harper Press.

Schechner, Richard. (1977, 2004) *Performance Theory*, London and New York: Routledge.

Sconce, Jeffrey. (2000) *Haunted Media*, Durham: Duke University Press.

——(2004) 'See You in Hell, Johnny Bravo!', in S. Murray and L. Ouellette (eds) *Reality TV: Remaking Television Culture*, New York: New York University Press: 432–59.

Scope Scholastic. (2010) 'Is Reality TV Making You Stupid?'. Accessed online: http://teacher.scholastic.com/scholasticnews/magazines/scope/pdfs/SCOPE-101110-EssayKit.pdf

Secondsync (2013) 'The X Factor', commercial report for social media, 16 December, internal publication.

——(2014a) 'Benefits Street', commercial report for social media, 20 January, internal publication.

——(2014b) 'TOWIE', commercial report for social media, 12 March, internal publication.

Sender, Katherine (2011) 'Real Worlds: Migrating Genres, Travelling Participants, Shifting Theories', in M. Kraidy and K. Sender (eds) (2011) *The Politics of Reality Television: Global Perspectives*, London and New York: Routledge: 1–11.

Sherwin, Adam. (2013) 'Viva Forever! Not Exactly', *Independent*, 2 May. Accessed online: www.theindependent.co.uk (accessed 3 July 2013).

Sinclair, Gary. (2014) 'Retreating Behind the Scenes: The "less"-Civilising Impact of Virtual Spaces on the Irish Heavy Metal Scene' in L. Duits, K. Zwaan and S. Reijnders (eds) (2014) *The Ashgate Research Companion to Fan Cultures*, London: Ashgate.

Skeggs, Beverley and Wood, Helen. (2012) *Reacting to Reality Television: Performance, Audience and Value*, London: Routledge.

Skeggs, Beverley, Wood, Helen and Thumin, Nancy. (2008) '"Oh My Goodness I Am Watching Reality TV": How Methodology Makes Class in Multi-Method Audience Research,' *European Journal of Cultural Studies*, 11(1): 5–24.

Stelter, Brian. (2012) 'Idol Grapples with its own Competition', *New York Times*, 22 May. Accessed online: www.nytimes.com/2012/05/23/arts/television/american-idol-ponders-a-ratings-dip-on-fox.html?_r=0.

Sukhadwala, Sejal. (2012) 'The Bogus Quest for "Authentic" Food', *Guardian*, 28 May. Accessed online: www.theguardian.com/lifeandstyle/wordofmouth/2012/may/28/bogus-quest-for-authentic-food.

Szerszynski, Bronislaw, Heim, Wallace and Waterton, Claire (eds). (2003) *Nature Performed: Environment, Culture and Performance*, Oxford: Blackwell.

Turner, Graeme. (2004) *Understanding Celebrity*, London: Sage.

Turner, Victor. (1986) *The Anthropology of Performance*, New York: PAJ.

Tyson Smith, R. (2008) 'Passion Work: The Joint Production of Emotional Labor in Professional Wrestling,' *Social Psychology Quarterly*, 71(2): 157–76.

Van Bauwel, Sofie and Carpentier, Nico. (2010) *Trans-reality Television: The Transgressions of Reality, Genre, Politics, and Audience*, Plymouth: Lexington Books/Rowman and Littlefield.

Watts, Amber. (2009) '"Melancholy, Merit and Merchandise": The Postwar Audience Participation Show', in S. Murray and L. Ouellette (eds) (2009) *Reality TV: Remaking Television Culture*, New York: New York University Press: 301–20.

Weber, Brenda. (2009) *Makeover TV: Selfhood, Citizenship, and Celebrity*, Durham and London: Duke University Press.

Whannel, Garry. (2007) *Culture, Politics and Sport: Blowing the Whistle, Revisited*, London: Routledge.

Wood, Douglas. (2013) 'Interview with Author', 16 August 2013.

Woods, Faye. (2012) 'Classed Femininity, Performativity, and Camp in British Structured Reality Programming', *Television and New Media*, 1–18.

Zelizer, Viviana. (2005) *The Purchase of Intimacy*, New York: Princeton University Press.

——(2013) *Economic Lives*, New York: Princeton University Press.

INDEX

12 Years a Slave 163
999 10–11, 24, 29, 34–5

A Very British Airline 9
A&E 4
Abercrombie, Nick 56, 145
affective economics 22, 85–6, 102
Ahtola, Dan 108–18, 134, 151, 152
Airline 33
Airport 28, 33, 60, 61–2
Aitkenhead, Decca 141–2
Allen, Robert C. 41, 86
AMC 6, 148, 164
America's Funniest Home Videos 30
America's Most Wanted 28, 30, 34
America's Next Top Model 62, 158
Andrejevic, Mark 65, 86, 130
Animal Hospital 24
audiences, fans and anti-fans 145;
    see also fans and anti-fans
authenticity 23, 69–70, 72, 58, 162–3

Baker, Stephanie Alice 115
Barthes, Roland 23, 105, 109–14, 122,
    124, 134, 150
Baudrillard, Jean 121, 123
Bazalgette, Peter 13, 38, 40
BBC 1–2, 9–11, 14–15, 24, 27–8, 30–1,
    33–8, 57, 60, 77, 82, 85, 121, 142, 147,
    149, 153
BBC Worldwide 2, 15, 120, 147
Becker, Karin 115
Beckham, David 88
Beekman, Scott M. 105–6, 116, 152
Benefits Street 141, 148
Bennington, Emily 128
Big Brother, 6, 10, 13, 21, 25–51,
    63–71, 76–8, 83–88, 97–9, 132,

149, 157–61; *Big Brother
    moment* 25
Bignell, Jonathan 7, 9, 140–41
Billington, Michael 144
Biltereyst, Daniel 128
binge fans 147–8
Biressi, Anita 65
Black, Benjamin 164
Bolin, Göran 4
Bonner, Frances 57
Boyle, Raymond 14–15, 80, 87–8, 91,
    110, 126
Boyle, Susan 16, 53, 74–5, 79, 142
Branche, Ruben 3
brands 138, 143
Brants, Kees 11
Breaking Bad 148
Brooker, Charlie 94, 125–6, 154
Brunsdon, C. 28
business reality television 13–15
Business Week 107

Calvert, Clay 66
Candid Camera 30
Cantrell, Tom 89
Carpentier, Nico 14, 85
Carter, Bill 5, 6
Carter, Gary 3, 7, 21, 23–5, 36, 38, 43–4,
    48–9, 53–4, 57–60, 64, 72–5, 137–8,
    156, 158–9, 161, 163
Cashmore, Ellis 88
Castaway 36–8
Catfish: The TV Show 160
celebrities 23, 94–103, 126
Celebrity Big Brother 95
Celebrity Boxing 105, 122
Celebrity Wrestling 121
Changing Rooms 30–1, 82

Channel 4 38, 40
Children's Hospital 35, 58
Coleman, Stephen 9, 132–4, 158–9
Collins, Suzanne 101
commercial television 36, 44, 50
competitive reality television 10, 21, 35, 51, 53, 69–71, 94, 121–2, 134–5, 156–7; as mega formats 79; audiences of 64; escalation of 23; target market of 68, 97–8
Corner, John 9, 11, 26, 42, 53, 70, 81, 90, 138, 156, 162
Coronation Street 86–7
Couldry, Nick 19
Craymer, Judy 16
cross-media content 5, 11, 13, 25, 75, 81, 138–39, 161
cultural performance 56, 105, 107–10, 117–18, 127, 132, 150, 155

Daily Mail 2, 40
Dancing with the Stars 15, 20, 147
Deery, June 11, 17, 76, 123–4
Delwiche, Aaron 122, 156
Dent, Grace 47
Deuze, Mark 156
documentary 57–8, 64, 89–90, 92; drama documentary 140; fly on the wall 57; observational 39, 59, 163
documusical 90, 92
Donovan, Julie 39, 50, 74, 100, 127, 159
Dovey, John 12, 120
Downton Abbey 4
Dr Who 138
Dragon's Den 14
drama 93, 117, 122, 125, 150, 163; drama documentary 140; multistage-drama 156–7; social drama 52, 67–8, 156
Driving School 30
Duck Dynasty 4, 9
Duits, Linda 130
Dunning, Eric 112, 126

E! 15, 75, 124
EastEnders 33, 86

economics: affective 22, 85–6; emotional 95–6, 113–14, 135, 138; political 7, 34
Educating Yorkshire 163
Elegy for April 164
Elias, Norbert 112, 126
emotional hub 90–1, 93
engagement 41, 68, 78, 82, 84, 90, 93–4, 111, 113, 129, 134, 136, 146–7, 149; audience engagement 22, 26, 53, 58, 77, 84, 102, 128, 134, 138, 147; consumer engagement 22, 102; emotional engagement 84, 87, 91, 93–5, 101, 164; modes of engagement 41, 92, 111, 113, 147, 149, 150–2, 155; negative engagement 94, 113, 150
entertainment formats 10, 13–14, 26, 137; creation of 29; markets for 82
Entertainment Weekly 6
Exit Through The Gift Shop 160
experience economy 22, 80–6, 102, 139

factual entertainment 9–11, 14–15, 21, 24–35, 40, 50, 59, 88, 153, 162; range of 29–33
fair treatment 101
Faking It 15, 123, 154
faking it, smart fans and marks 114, 128
fans and anti-fans 40, 67, 100, 104, 111–14, 133, 136, 145–50, 152
Faulks, Sebastian 16
fiction 22, 89, 138, 159
Ford, Sam 121
Fox News 17
Freeman, Martin 4
FremantleMedia 1, 5, 54
Full Metal Jousting 123

Gallagher, William 38
Game of Thrones 147
Gauntlett, David 28, 41
Geordie Shore 125–6, 128
George, Bill 162
Gilmore, James 80–1, 83

Giuffre, Liz 113
Glynn, Kevin 11, 82, 130, 131
Goffman, Erving 21, 52–6, 60,
    69–70, 155
Gogglebox 47
Gray, Jonathan 113, 148
Grindstaff, Laura 53
Guardian 4, 44, 77

Halperin, Shirley 5
Haunted 6
Haynes, Richard 80, 87–8, 91, 111, 126
HBO 147
Hearn, Alison 85
Hell on Wheels 164
Hell's Kitchen 13
Henricks, Thomas 112
Here Comes Honey Boo Boo 94–5,
    143, 154
Heritage, Stuart 2, 44, 77, 123
Herman, James 73
Hermes, Joke 19–20, 148
Hibberd, James 2, 6
Hill, Annette 2, 4, 11, 12–13, 15, 18, 20,
    28, 34, 36, 39, 41, 67–8, 77, 82–3, 117,
    140, 148
Hill, Harry 55, 144
Hills, Matt 147
Hobson, Dorothy 41
Hochschild, Arlie 11, 124, 139, 147
Hollender, Pål 143
Holmes, Su 13, 57–8
House of Cards 148
Household, N. 58
Hyde, Marina 51

I Can't Sing! The X Factor Musical 16,
    54–5, 144–5
I Dreamed a Dream 16, 53
I'm a Celebrity ... Get Me Out Of Here!
    2, 4, 13, 95, 96, 122–3, 142
Imre, Aniko 126
infotainment 10–11, 21, 24, 50, 82, 98,
    153, 162
intergeneric space 142

Jackson, Randy 73, 159
Jacobs Henderson, Jennifer 121, 156
James, William 116
Jenkins, Henry 85
Jermyn, Deborah 13
Jerry Springer 115, 131
Jersey Shore 17, 32, 124, 128
Johnson, Angela 40

Kaufman, Seth 3, 16
Kautsky, Robert 115
Kavka, Misha 43, 61, 97, 158
Keeping Up with the Kardashians 15, 75,
    94, 124–5, 132, 154; Kardashian,
    Khloe 124; Kardashian, Kim 124;
    Kardashian, Kourtney 124;
    Kardashian, Rob 15
Kelly, Diedre 142
Kelly, Lisa 14–15
Kerrick, George, E. 115
Kilborn, Richard 12, 33–5, 39, 53, 58, 60,
    88–90
Kraidy, Marwan 7, 13, 20, 26

Lawson, Mark 3, 6, 150, 158
Ledet, Joshua 73
Lehane, Denis 3
Levi, Heather 106–9, 116–17, 150
Life of Grime 70
lifestyle and makeover television 30–1
light entertainment 57, 58, 140
Lindsay 96
Lindsay, Jeff 137
Lion Television 37
Lipkin, Steve, N. 89
Living With the Enemy 89
Lohan, Lindsay 9, 96
Longhurst, Brian 56, 145, 146
lucha libre 104, 106–7, 108, 115, 150
Luckhurst, Mary 89
Lunt, Peter 115–16
Lury, Karen 7
magical entertainment 117
Maguire, Brendan 107
Malone, Gareth 3

Mamma Mia 16
Mark Burnett Productions 13
MasterChef 3, 10, 13, 16
Mathijs, Ernest 11, 65
Mayer, Vicki 100
McCall, Davina 63
McCarthy, Anna 30
McGrath, John, E. 53, 66–7, 72, 79, 161
McQueen, Steve 164
media event 13
melodrama 43
Mesnick, Jason 17
Meyrowitz, Joshua 53, 70, 145, 155
Mikos, Lothar 69
Military Wives 3
Mills, Jeremy 37, 60
Mob Wives 15, 123
Moonlight Mile 3
MTV's The Real World 12, 32, 82, 153
multiple realities 139
Murray, Susan 13

Napoli, Phillip 80, 82, 84, 146
Nationwide 30
Neale, Steve 50
Nelson, Scott A. 34
Netflix 27, 148
New York Times, The 5, 6
news 11, 30–1, 153
Nichols, Bill 31, 64
Norris, Chris 17
Nunn, Heather 65

O'Connell, Michael 4, 125
ordinary people 43
Oren, Tasha 13
Orwell, George 64
Ouellette, Laurie 7, 13, 26
OWN 96

Paddington Green 33
Paget, Derek 90, 92, 140
Palahniuk, Chuck 6
Palin, Michael 3
participation 57

passion 22–3, 87–8, 91, 102, 106,
    111–16, 124, 150, 152
Peaky Blinders 164
People magazine 17
performance 54
performance of the self 21, 42, 52–4, 56,
    74, 77, 94, 96, 100, 142, 146, 155–60
performing power 132
Petridis, Alex 144
Piazza, Jo 17
Pine, Joseph 80–1, 83
Police, Camera, Action! 29, 31
politics of reality television 26,
Poniewozik, James 2
Pop Idol 5, 10, 17, 25, 54, 76
Popstars 158
Powell, R 34
Press Association 144–5
Price, Gareth 141
producing authenticity 162
professional wrestling 104, 107, 109,
    114, 134, 150–2
public and popular 33
public service television 44, 33–36, 48

Raffel, Stanley 60
Raphael, Chad 12, 28–9, 34
RDF Media 154
real people as entertainment 47
reality and sports entertainment 104
reality bites 137
reality entertainment 119
reality television contestants 94–5, 97,
    100, 142, 158; celebrity contestants 95
reality television performers 93–4, 97
reality TV before *Big Brother* 27
reality TV 1, 3–6, 7, 9, 12–30, 36, 38, 47,
    50–4, 58, 61, 65–6, 72, 76; 66; anti-
    reality TV 148, 150; as a cultural
    phenomenon 21; audience research
    18–20; as intergeneric space 1, 9–10,
    129, 138–9, 164; branding 76; cultural
    value 95, 126, 128; definitions 9–18;
    economics 22, 34, 95–6, 102, 139,
    160; history of 30, 39, 48, 50–1, 139;

reality television and surveillance 53; spectacle of 121, 122
Redhead, Steve 127
Reijnders, Stijn 130
Rescue 911 10, 28, 34
Rojek, Chris 96
Roscoe, Jane 6, 66–7, 69–71, 74–5, 77, 131, 138, 157, 162–4
Ross, Karen 19
Rowe, David 115

Sandvoss, Cornell 147
Sassoon, Donald 30, 138
Saunders, Jennifer 16
SBS 6
Schechner, Richard 55–6, 107, 150
Sconce, Jeffrey 12, 122, 131
Scope Scholastic 128–9
Sender, Katherine 7, 13, 20, 26, 15
Shahaf, Sharen 13
Sherlock 4
Sherwin, Adam 16
Shine Group 3, 24, 40, 53, 73, 91, 98, 143
Shipwrecked 38
Skeggs, Beverly 53, 78–9, 100, 126
smart fans and marks 114, 128, 130, 135, 154–5
soap opera 9, 12–13, 33, 39, 41–3, 51, 67, 86, 106, 115, 138
social media 22, 102, 136, 167
soft scripted reality television 143
spectacle of excess 23, 104, 112, 122, 125, 128, 135, 150–2, 162
spectacle/performance paradigm 145
spectacular entertainment 108, 121
Splash! 2
sports 87–88, 91, 102, 109, 113, 119
sports entertainment 22, 23, 103–8, 110–14, 116, 119–20, 126, 129, 131–2, 137, 150–2, 154
staged event 39
Steemers, Jeanette 13, 83
Stelter, Brian 5
Stenner, Paul 115–16
Streetmate 63

Strictly Come Dancing 2, 10, 15, 36, 53, 77, 82–3, 121, 147, 154–5
Sukhadwala, Sejal 162
surveillance culture 64–7
Survivor 4, 6, 10, 13, 16, 25, 35–6, 157
Sverige Idol 17
Sylvania Waters 32

The American Family 32
The Apprentice 13, 15
The Bachelor 17, 143
The Bachelorette 17
The Hotel 149
The Hunger Games 101, 122, 128, 142, 150
The King of Pain 16
The Office 142, 149
The Truman Show 156
The Voice 26, 77, 80, 85
The Walking Dead 6
TLC 95, 143
Turner, Victor 56, 107, 150
TV4 14, 17
Tyson Smith, R. 116, 152

US Weekly 17

Van Bauwel, Sofie 14
VH1 15, 120
Viva Forever! 16
voyeurs and viewers 64

Watts, Amber 57
West, Amy 43
Whannel, Gary 87
Widholm, Andreas 115
Wife Swap 78, 122, 126
Wood, Douglas 40, 44, 47–8, 73, 77, 98, 142, 159
Wood, Helen 53, 78–9, 100, 126
Woods, Faye 126
World Wrestling Entertainment 106–8, 114, 116, 152

Zelizer, Viviana 8
Zwaan, Koos 130